DEAR YOUNG SPARROW

by Cally Logan

For Anna Reinstein, the teacher who inspired me to find my voice in writing.

For Mom and Dad, for loving me for who I am.

And most truly,

All honor, glory, and praise to Jesus Christ, to Whom all credit is due.

Contents

Introduction

Chapter I: Radical

Chapter II: Mirror, Mirror

Chapter III: Teammates

Chapter IV: School

Chapter V: Dating

Chapter VI: Pretty Little Fools

Chapter VII: Active Waiting

Chapter VIII: Back to God

Chapter IX: Bloomed

Chapter X: The One

Introduction

'Sup

Where to begin a book? Well. I could start off standing upon a little soap box pouring out my heart, I could start in a gentle whisper and then end off loud (*Les Miserables* style of course) or I could speak to you like I would if you and I were at a coffee shop. See, though I do not know you personally, young sparrow, I consider you a friend. Matthew 10 shares how He knows every sparrow, and reader, He knows you. I hope as you pick up this book or kindle or iPad it feels like a very warm handshake. I hope these words ahead feel warm and embracing, but never judgmental. I pray you feel so rest assured that the chapters to come have been heavily prayed upon and ample time in the Word has been spent upon these revelations and convictions. In truth, I feel guilty even placing my name on the cover. You see, it is really the Holy Spirit of God prompting me to write. I feel at times like a little monkey hitting away at the keys of this MacBook while He guides me. I say this, because in this world we need to be smart. 1 John 4 speaks of testing the spirits, and that is more real than we realize. If we are going to take time to listen to someone, we need to know that they are Biblically sound. This requires the correct balance of Scripture and Spirit, and that is something I adamantly pursue, especially in this book.

So, make some tea and let's have a little chat......

Chapter I: Radical

Live Rad

"By this everyone will know that you are my disciples, if you love one another." -John 13:35

What does it really mean to be a Christian? What is the difference between a Christian and a follower of Christ? The answer is how you live. A Christian is someone who has accepted into their hearts and minds that Jesus is the Son of God, but a follower of Christ has accepted this and chooses to live out a life imitating Christ. This means living out a life in such a way that people can tell you are set apart, you are living as Christ called all of us to live. This is represented most by how we love. Now, even those who are not followers of Christ can love someone else. Love is best defined as someone who, "puts another person before himself." What if we radically took that to a next level? To a Christ follower level? What if we chose to not live in even the mainstream of Church culture, and we actually lived as Christ did?

This would require stepping out of our comfort zones. Suddenly keeping to our safe Christian circles of friends would be challenged as we chose to sit with people who aren't saved, people who don't live perfectly, even the outcasts. Jesus did this plain and simple, at the time he chose to sit with tax collectors (unpopular in any time) and even women who sold themselves for money. Now, what is important is to realize Jesus never said what they did was acceptable, nor did He participate in their sins, but He radically loved and accepted them as people who needed a friend. How can we imitate Christ in this? Perhaps we can sit with that coworker who always sits alone. Perhaps we can start up a conversation with someone who doesn't look a thing like us. Perhaps we can love radically.

I had the honest blessing of having a very outcast spirit. I admit it and own it with a bit of pride that I am very different from everyone. I don't really fall into a certain mold of how I dress, speak, or act. That being said, my "people" are usually those who perk up at the mention of Star Wars or a historical event, or a pop-punk band of the OO's. I honestly would not change a thing about myself in that manner, for it allows me to connect and engage with others on many levels and provides the blessing and opportunity to love them. It honestly breaks my heart seeing what a skewed and wrong perception most people have about Christians.

Gandhi said, "I like your Christ, but not your Christians" and that vividly spoke to me. I am in no way bashing Church culture, but I am saying that it is time that we break that mold and stereotype that Christians are bigots who judge others and misrepresent the name of Christ. It is time we step out and live radically just as Jesus did. It is time we love others and embrace them in love, not condemning or affirming their actions, but merely loving them as children of God.

Living radically also means we live differently than society, or even Church culture. We uphold what Christ calls us to do, like keeping Sundays holy, or tithing. It means waiting to have sex until marriage, and placing a high value on marriage in the first place. It means picking up our cross and following

His lead, even if it looks dangerous and terrifying. Christ never once said that He would call us to live in secure little bubbles on Comfort Zone Island. He called us to trust Him and be different.

Our society oddly enough highlights often how great it is to be different, so what if we actually lived like Jesus calls us to live? What if we took the first ten minutes of our mornings and read the Word and His Own words, rather than scroll through Facebook? What if we didn't conform to the ways of this world, and we wholly ran after Him, not worrying about reputations or the thoughts of others, but truly just caring about what He thinks of us? What if we lived radically and pursued a life after Him? What if we turned these, "what ifs" into actions and actually did? That is what this book is about. Learning and striving to live radically different from what society and even misguided aspects of Church culture Pharisees demand, and choosing to pick up your cross and follow Christ daily. Are you ready, young sparrow?

Prayer:

Dear Lord,

Thank You. Thank You for giving us such a beautiful example of how to live and how we can best serve You. Lord, please ever mold our hearts to Your desires and Your will, so that we may live in such an abundance. Please guide our hearts to be steadfast and radically bold, stepping out to not merely confess You as Lord, but to take up our own crosses and follow You.

In Your name,
Amen.

Who God Is

My youth director when I was a teen said something that has stuck with me over a decade, "If you are going to spend all of eternity with God, shouldn't you know more of Who He is?" This hit the marrow, but I did not fully understand it until later. It's a continuous process. As Christians we get so stuck on desiring to know the Will of God, but wouldn't it be easier to understand His Will if we understood more of Who He is?

The Bible is the only source of absolute truth we have, and in this God breathed Word we can find answers. He can speak through a verse or story. This is what the Bible shares on just a glimpse of the character of God:

Hebrews 13:8 "Jesus Christ is the same yesterday and today and forever."

1 John 4:8, "Anyone who does not love does not know God, because God is love."

Job 12:7-10, ""But ask the beasts, and they will teach you; the birds of the heavens, and they will tell you; or the bushes of the earth, and they will teach you; and the fish of the sea will declare to you. Who among all these does not know that the hand of the Lord has done this? In his hand is the life of every living thing and the breath of all mankind."

John 15:1-27, ""I am the true vine, and my Father is the vinedresser. Every branch in me that does not bear fruit he takes away, and every branch that does bear fruit he prunes, that it may bear more fruit. Already you are clean because of the word that I have spoken to you. Abide in me, and I in you. As the branch cannot bear fruit by itself, unless it abides in the vine, neither can you, unless you abide in me. I am the vine; you are the branches. Whoever abides in me and I in him, he it is that bears much fruit, for apart from me you can do nothing."

1 Samuel 15:29, "He who is the Glory of Israel does not lie or change his mind; for he is not a human being, that he should change his mind."

From just a glimpse of these few verses the truth is we don't even begin to scratch the surface of God. He is infinite and omnipotent, He is everywhere, and over every single thing, but in seeking Him more deeply, we can come to know Him through our lives. One of the most important verses listed about is the one of first Samuel of how God is not a man that He should lie, nor change His mind. This is evident through many stories of women in the Bible.

Hannah was the mother of Samuel and first hand saw the character of God through a promise. She was barren and ashamed. She so desperately desired a child to bless her husband, but also to know her God better at the same time. The interlinear translation shares that Hannah, "copiously wept" for this desperate prayer. God spoke a promise through a prophecy unto her and kept the promise. That is the key-God kept His word. To a woman literally mocked for being so barren, He kept the promise. Hannah rejoiced in this. Not merely because she saw the fulfillment of this promise literally born through a child, but because she knew with no shadow or hint of doubt that the God she served was faithful, loving, merciful, and cared about her. She could stand all the days of her life knowing full well that her God was faithful. The direct translation of the song she wrote to the Lord in thanksgiving is incredible:

"My heart has exulted in God; my horn is lifted high in God. My mouth has been large over my enemies; for I have rejoiced in Your salvation. There is none holy like Jehovah, for there is none except You: yea, there is no rock like our God." (1 Samuel 2).

This is a woman who knows Who her God is. Now the caveat to this is that there were seasons that were rough for her. Coming to know the true character of God more often than not requires a season in which there is an issue, and trust must be built and made in Him. For many in the Bible and beyond, it may be a promise, or it may be a problem. The glorious thing about God is that He is never changing, so all that is true for those in the Bible is true for us today. John shares in the final chapter of his Gospel that if he were to share all that Christ did on this earth, "Jesus did many other things as well. If every one of them were written down, I suppose that even the whole world would not have room for the books that would be written." (John 21:25). We serve an unchanging God, so do not believe for one second that we forfeit anything just because we don't live in the years the Bible was recorded.

Another story of a mighty woman that trusted God and saw fulfillment and His true character was that of Elizabeth. She was the mother of John the Baptist. Elizabeth was well beyond the years in which she should be able to have a child, but the Lord sent an Angel to her husband to tell him that indeed they would have a son. Elizabeth believed this, she held firm to it. In due time, she and Zachariah did indeed conceive a child and her response is incredible, "Blessed is she who has believed that the Lord would fulfill his promises to her!'" (Luke 1:45). When she said this as well, it was to encourage Mary. Mary, the mother of Christ.... let's take a moment to completely let that sink in that God showed His true character in a promise and fulfillment to one woman, and that woman encouraged the mother of Christ in her own promise. That is what fellowship is, encouraging one another in Christ and Who He is. DT Niles says, "Christianity is one beggar telling another beggar where he found bread."

To bring this back around, let us seek Him. Let us seek Him to find Him and to know Him well. Matthew 7:7 says, "Ask and it will be given to you; seek and you will find; knock and the door will be opened to you." The fact of the matter is albeit the promises given to the women mentioned here and to others through the span of history were fulfilled, they are merely bonuses in reality. The greatest and most glorious gift of all is knowing more deeply Who the Creator truly is, His faithfulness and His never-ending love. The greatest blessing of all time is knowing and standing upon such promises and ebenezers so that no matter what may befall in life, there is a firm and secure anchor in knowing Who He is, and that indeed all things are woven and worked together for His glory and our benefit. Let us rejoice in that promise of Romans 8:28, and indeed go forth to invoke and seek Him to reveal His character to us. After all, if we are to spend all of eternity with Him, it would be nice to know Him as well as we can.

Prayer:

Dear Lord Jesus,

Thank You for your enduring and loving grace. We pray that through the course of trials and lessons we learn throughout our lives that You would be glorified through the constant theme of Your faithfulness and mercy. We pray that You would anchor us and work deeply in us so that we could come to know You better. We pray that just as Elizabeth saw Your glory manifested in a fulfilled promise, that we would not shy away from instances that You would provide for such great promises, such great faith, and such great miracles.

In Your name,
Amen.

Off the Cuff Moment

So, I like to take these moments just to have little odd stories or things. So, in the 1990's Chuck E. Cheese's was **far** different than it is today. Chuck E. looked like a literal rat, not a cute little mouse like he is pictured today. Anyway, way back in 1994 there was a splendid little birthday party for a little girl named, Cally. Well, Cally loved Chuck E. Cheese's, but was deathly afraid of Chuck E., who appeared as a vile, sewer dweller wearing a large bowtie. Cally's parents assured her that Chuck E. would not appear in the flesh, so not to be alarmed or dismayed. As the story goes, the hokey-pokey arose and of course as birthday girl, Cally was the caboose of the capricious occasion, but who is to appear right behind Cally? None other than the verminous six-foot-tall party animal himself than Chuck E. And that my friends, is why Cally is who she is today.

Build Your Relationship Now!

Today marks a very special day, why you ask? Well, today is the seven-year mark since God revealed a very special promise to me. The catch of it all is, God did not give it to me right away, quite the contrary in fact. It would be a long and growing haul; a promise much like that given to Abraham to wait for, trust God for, and to trust why the answer of, "wait" was sufficient. God knew what was best. You see, God had bigger plans for me than I even had for myself. That all came about from building my relationship with God more single.

The goal of a relationship with God is not at all to get a marriage as a gift, but a marriage can be blessed more by a good relationship with God. The more we seek His face, the more we find the living water that satisfies our souls. Jeremiah 33:3 says, "'Call to me and I will answer you and tell you great and unsearchable things you do not know.' Our lives are marked by great unknowns and questions that we frequently ponder, yet more often than not we rely too heavily on our own strengths to find them out. More often than not, we end up with even more questions and less answers.

Society has taught us that in order to be functional adults we must be completely self-sufficient and reliant upon our own strengths, yet that only yields a perfectionist complex marked with overwhelming impossibilities to actually live up to such a demand. We buy into the lie that everyone else has all of their crap together, and we are the only ones who don't. We buy into the lie that somehow, we are the only ones insecure on this planet. What if for even just a few minutes we took off the facade that we can do this by ourselves, and realized our deep need for a Savior? Christ wants to take that on, and He wants to walk with you in your life. Not just the milestones, but every single step. I kid you not, I even ask Him to direct the hairdresser when I get my hair colored sometimes!

Matthew 11:30 says, "For My yoke is easy and My burden is light." What Jesus is saying here, is that He actually wants your crap. He wants your good, your bad, your ugly. He wants to walk this path with you, and actually work even the bad and ugly things out for your favor. The thing is, that takes a relationship with Him.

I've come to hate the correlation of being a follower of Christ with the word, "religion." The dictionary defines religion as, "a set of beliefs concerning the cause, nature, and purpose of the universe, especially when considered as the creation of a superhuman agency or agencies, usually involving devotional and ritual observances, and often containing a moral code governing the conduct of human affairs." This sounds so much like a strict club with impossible rules. What it lacks entirely is the relationship aspect with Christ. Religion will tell you what to do, when to do it, and how to do it, and if you mess up, how to atone for your sin. Beyond that, you're alone in a vast universe with no real crutch or friend to rely on. Being a follower of Christ entails a relationship with Him, built on His faithfulness and His love. You in turn find yourself wanting to follow the laws in the Bible, because of that love found in Christ. It isn't out of guilt that you are dutiful, it is out of love for God. More so, when you do fail to meet expectations as you will as a human, He freely forgives you. Because of the relationship aspect, you don't want to do it again, because you don't want to let Him down again. That is unlike any "religion" or collective practice any human could ever possibly just dream up.

So how does one really dig in and build a relationship with God? Honestly, it starts with honest and vulnerable prayer. The kind of prayer where you do come before Him with reverence and respect, but you are raw, honest, and real with Him. He knows anyway, you won't surprise Him with anything He doesn't already know. What comes next is getting to know Him through His book. John 1 shares, "In the beginning was the Word, and the Word was with God, and the Word was God. He was with God in the beginning. Through him all things were made; without him nothing was made that has been made. In him was life, and that life was the light of all mankind. The light shines in the darkness, and the darkness has not overcome it." We can come to know Him better by His breathed Word. This Word is something of the most value, for in our hands we can tangibly hold the only absolute truth on the planet. Also, in this Word, we can come to know His character, faithfulness, miracles, and His love. The Bible is the sole book the reader can pick up and feel loved by the author.

Community comes into play next. As a follower of Christ, we are the church. We are called to meet together, worship together, share burdens and blessings together, and to work together as a team for Him. Prayerfully seeking a good Bible based church is vital to your relationship with God. God will use His children often too to speak to you! The pertinent thing here is to get into a church that is solidly rooted in the Word and the truth.

Most of all, it's the day to day. Paul calls for believers to, "pray without ceasing." This can be different at first, but when put into practice, will become as natural as breathing. Take a day and anytime you find yourself with a free thought, pray it out. Talk to God about that person at school that was bothering you. Talk to Him about how to handle friends, guys, your parents. Your greatest and strongest relationship should be with God, and like all relationships, that requires getting to know the other person and communication. He will speak back to you in an abundance of ways, you just have to listen.

So, work on your relationship with Him now when you are young, for when life gets harder, or when life gets bigger, you'll have Him right there with you.

Prayer:

Dear Lord,

We thank You for your love and for Who You are. We pray that You would overwhelm us with Your enduring and loving Holy Spirit. We invite you in this very moment into our lives, hearts, circumstances, and days. We pray that Your love would cover us like a fresh blanket of snow, not leaving even a fragment of our lives untouched by You. We pray for a deeper knowledge and relationship with You, so that we may come to know you better on this side of the veil.

In Your name we pray,

Amen.

Learning to Trust

How often do we say, "I trust God" to others, but in all truthfulness, we are scared out of our minds and holding to hope that He somehow might actually come through, but just in case we are guarding up our hearts? We are beginning to lay those bricks up to create walls around our hearts, separating us from God because we think there is that chance that He won't actually come through. I think it's about time that we become honest with ourselves and with God and say, "I'm learning to trust You, God." This is honest, and it is ok to say. He knows it, and honestly a deeper relationship can be formed when we are honest with Him rather than putting up fallacies blockading the truth.

CS Lewis said, "We are not necessarily doubting that God will do the best for us; we are wondering how painful the best will turn out to be." When God calls us to do a mission or task, it is rarely without endurance and pain. We tend to doubt His goodness and His love and fall into not trusting Him when those challenges spring up in front of us. Lack of trust comes from fear. This is why it is honestly good to be honest with God during these times when we don't trust Him. One of the greatest examples of this can be seen in the Bible when Jesus calms the storm. If you do not know the story, it can be found in Mark 4:35-41,

"That day when evening came, he said to his disciples, "Let us go over to the other side." Leaving the crowd behind, they took him along, just as he was, in the boat. There were also other boats with him. A furious squall came up, and the waves broke over the boat, so that it was nearly swamped. Jesus was in the stern, sleeping on a cushion. The disciples woke him and said to him, "Teacher, don't you care if we drown?"

He got up, rebuked the wind and said to the waves, "Quiet! Be still!" Then the wind died down and it was completely calm.

He said to his disciples, "Why are you so afraid? Do you still have no faith?"

They were terrified and asked each other, "Who is this? Even the wind and the waves obey him!"

Even Jesus's team was terrified and did not trust Him in this example. Recall here that these men had seen countless healings, miracles, and wonders while following Him. Many of them also were skilled fishermen, so the seas were nothing new to them, but this was one heck of a storm. They glanced over to see Jesus sleeping, unafraid and unbothered by the storm, yet they ran around like chickens with their heads cut off. They didn't trust Him for those moments. They finally woke Jesus up and begged Him to save them, and his response was, "do you still have no faith?" We can relate to the disciples here. So often we get caught up in the storms that we don't actually trust Him to get us to the other side.

So, what do we do? Do we side idly during the storms and ignore them? Or do we actually admit that we are learning to trust God and leave it there at the cross? Being honest with God is exactly what we need to do. Not one of us are perfect, if we were and had spotless faith what would the real need for a Savior be? If we could save ourselves, why then would we need to put our faith in a High Power? In no way am I saying that through every storm we should doubt and lose faith or trust, but it is ok to be learning throughout. Storms build endurance, so over time we become stronger in Him. Suddenly what was a hurricane in the past is now nothing more than a drizzling shower. What is key being that we are learning, just as the disciples were learning. We are learning to trust God and we are learning more about His character with each day. We are learning that we are flawed humans in desperate need of a Savior, and we are learning that He doesn't just love us, He actually likes us and has what's best for us in store.

Prayer:

Dear Lord,

You know our hearts and minds. Help us to be more honest and vulnerable with You, so that we may come into a deeper relationship with you. Please teach us more of your character so that we may grow in our faith and relationships with you, so that when storms come we may not fear and we may come into a deeper trust in You. We love You and in earnest desire to trust and not fear, but when our faith has holes, please work in us to fill them. Please bring us into a deeper understanding of You and Your plans for us that glorify You and benefit us.

In Jesus name,

Amen.

Surrender and the Key to Happiness

There is a common fallacy that we allow our prideful flesh to buy into, that "surrender" is death. In reality, yes, it is death, but perhaps not all death is a bad thing. Perhaps death to self can actually be the key that unlocks truly living. Stick with me now....

When we are young society tells us that the only way to success and happiness is independence. We live in a country literally built on the concept of being independent, and the American Dream is in itself really self-sufficiency and reliance. Being independent is not completely a bad thing, we do not want to remain in an infant state needing someone else to clean up our messes and perform everything for us, but complete independence is a date for jaded loneliness. The concept of the world being rested upon our shoulders with no one or nothing to help support it will only lead to a crumbling. This is why we need to be interdependent. We need a Savior. It is plain and simple really, we need a Higher Power to help direct our paths and kiss our boo boos at times. We need an ally of Higher Power Who actually gives a hoot about us. We need Jesus. But in this need for Jesus we must die of ourselves. Romans 8:13 says, "For if you live according to the flesh, you will die; but if by the Spirit you put to death the misdeeds of the body, you will live." Likewise, Luke 9:23 says, "And He was saying to them all, "If anyone wishes to come after Me, he must deny himself, and take up his cross daily and follow Me. "For whoever wishes to save his life will lose it, but whoever loses his life for My sake, he is the one who will save it."

In dying to our flesh, we are actually allowing the Spirit within us to completely come alive. When we stop fearing this death, we stop fearing life. We can live, and we have that backing that Jesus actually does have our back. Isaiah 48:17 says, "I am the Lord your God, Who teaches you what is best for you, Who directs you in the way that you should go." When we seek God, He actually has our best. When we die to our own wills and selfish ambitions, He actually blesses us. Think of it this way, Psalm 37:4 says, "Delight yourself in the Lord, and He will give you the desires of your heart." So, the pertinent piece of that verse is that when we delight in Him, or indwell and allow Him to move in our hearts, He places seeds. He fulfills His will, so those seeds will grow and prosper, and you will be not only blessed with that fruit, but your relationship with Him will become your true delight. Isaiah 49:23 shares, "Those who hope in the Lord will not be disappointed." This isn't to say that dying to yourself and delighting in the Lord is a straight shot to blessings and joy. In reality, the path is often extremely steep and hard. What it is to say is that in the end you won't be disappointed. In the end that surrender will bring you to the truest and purest joy and happiness, which is Christ Himself. John Piper coined it well, "He is most glorified when we are most satisfied in Him." We aren't disappointed when we are walking in highest satisfaction in Him. This doesn't come from the "stuff" He gives us, rather the immeasurably glorious joy that comes from loving Him *and* being loved in return. Suddenly even the long and tedious paths He calls us to become worth it. Suddenly the let downs of the flesh become meaningless. Suddenly the blessings become icing on the cake, but the true reward and the true substance is God. He is the reward, He is the delight, He is what makes all of life's hardships worth it.

So perhaps surrender isn't a bad thing after all. Perhaps it is in surrender that we truly find what it is to live and be happy. Of personal experience, it is only when I surrender something at the cross completely (and typically soaked in tears) that the clearest answers flood back. God delights in doing good for His kids, and you are counted in that group. Maybe that white flag is the thing we need to signify that we are indeed ready to be made clean at last.

Prayer:

Dear Lord,

Thank You for being the God that waits for us patiently, but also the God Who helps us to have the proper reason to know when we need to surrender. Help us Lord, to surrender. Help us to put down our own selfish pride and rest in the drenching and resting grace that is Your Holy Spirit.

In Jesus name,

Amen.

Chapter II: Mirror, Mirror

Who Do You Think You Are?

This chapter is going to be a little different, more of a questionnaire. For the following questions, I want you to read one, then think. Don't you dare gloss over this or read them super fast, instead treat each one as a piece of Godiva chocolate to be savored and considered. Ask yourself, ask God, ask others the answers. If you are reading this as a study, be vulnerable in your group and answer honestly. The point of this is to help develop yourself image, for before we can even get into deeper aspects of your life, you need to know who you are and what you stand for. So, have fun, be pensive, GO!

1) What is the most important thing to me in the world?

2) What do I think about most?

3) Who do I most admire to be like and why?

4) Do I believe what I believe because of my parents, because of my peers, or because it is what is real and has been revealed to me?

5) Are there gaps in my worldview or faith that I need to ask?

6) Do I believe God cares about me, loves me, and actually likes me?

7) Does my life reflect what I just answered to the previous question?

8) Who am I surrounding myself with?

9) Do these people make me the best version of me, or do they pull me down or into sin?

10) What is my best characteristic?

11) What is my worst characteristic?

12) What do I want my life to look like in 10 years?

13) What is my goal in life?

14) What am I striving towards as of now?

15) Do I spend more time lifting others up, or pulling them down?

16) What must I do to achieve my goals in the future?

17) Do I believe God has a steady hand upon my life?

18) What makes me happier than anything?

19) What brings the most sorrow to me?

20) What are things that calm me down?

21) What makes me the most anxious?

22) What is my worst nightmare?

23) What is my best daydream?

24) Am I beautiful?

25) What would I define as beautiful?

26) Am I successful?

27) What do I define as success?

28) Am I funny?

29) How would I define my humor?

30) Am I fun to be around?

31) Am I a reflection of Christ, a follower of Him?

32) Am I guilty as ever coming off as judgmental and not very Christian?

33) Do I speak kindness?

34) Do I have courage?

35) Am I healthy?

36) What would I define as healthy?

37) Am I more introverted or extroverted?

38) What are my best skills?

39) What skills need improvement?

40) Where do I feel called in the Body of Christ?

41) What do I feel my mission on earth is?

42) Where is my relationship with God?

43) What steps could I take to make my relationship with Him even better?

44) How well do I know God?

45) What are the main things I dwell upon daily?

46) How can I attain peace under chaos?

47) What can I be thankful for today?

48) What do I hope to learn in this book?

49) What do I hope to discover about myself in this book?

50) Am I happy?

Don't Compare Where You Are to Others

I just recently attended a wedding for my good friend's younger brother...younger by nearly four years. The other week I received a baby shower invitation for a friend expecting twins with her husband of nearly three years. My close friend was just promoted to management and makes nearly double what I do as a teacher. It is very easy to compare yourself to others, to compare where you are, or where you're going with those surrounding you. Believe it or not, it's ok not to be where all your friends are at the moment.

There's a chance you're like me and single at 25 making less than desirable. There's a chance you're like my close friend, Charlotte, and climbing that incredible corporate ladder and reaching amazing career goals. Or perhaps you're like my friend, Brianna, married to her college sweetheart for years or Tayla planning for twin boys with her husband. We all have different stories, but there is something kind of amazing about that. Romans 8:28 is a classic coffee mug verse, but that doesn't make it any less true. It shares, "And we know that in all things God works for the good of those who love him, who have been called according to his purpose." But what does this mean for you?

Romans 8:28 honestly should be the tagline of the entire Bible. That or John 13:7, "Jesus replied,

"You do not realize now what I am doing, but later you will understand." Both verses share the truth, we do not understand why things are the way that they are for us, but they are in fact an incredible blessing. Psalm 139 shares,

> "My frame was not hidden from you
> when I was made in the secret place,
> when I was woven together in the depths of the earth.
> Your eyes saw my unformed body;
> all the days ordained for me were written in your book
> before one of them came to be."

God knows what He is doing in your life, because every single day was planned before you came to even be knit together. Isn't that a comfort? The days we spend crying alone in the corner of our closets or in the parking lot of the gym screaming at Him are constructive because we are pressing harder into Him, but He sees the whole picture. He sees the beginning and the end. As cliché as it is, that coined term, "when everything is falling apart, it is actually falling together" is true. He has a plan for all the good and bad to work out for your benefit, but even better His glory.

People have a trend of putting on masks that everything is perfect and amazing, but deep down are screaming within over something not being great. Life will never be perfect, but we can come to a point of gratitude for the things that are right in life every day. Some days are harder than others to find this joy, but it is possible. For me, I long to be a wife and mother, and wear cute little dresses, and make pies for my husband, and play outside with my kids watching clouds every day, but instead I am doing something else. That is ok, for I know this is where God has me for today. Where you are right now is where God ordained for you to be, and it is where you can serve Him best in this moment. Do you ever see the time, 11:11 on your phone? Did you know those numbers have significance? It actually means you are right where you should be at that moment. It's like a God wink that you're where you should be right then.

It becomes easy to compare ourselves with one another in a world with so much social media. I won't be one of these authors who gets up on a soap box to condemn social media for its perfectionist flaws, but it does create a facade of the truth. That picture-perfect moment was probably one of 50 selfies taken with frowns in-between. Girls always suck in before a picture for a more svelte figure, and the perfect angle can make even a butt like a board look like Kim K. Perhaps if we spend less time comparing ourselves to each other, and more time being real and raw, we could finally get somewhere. That human element would finally shine through and we could all agree that we are broken humans, imperfect in every way, and so desperately in need of love and acceptance. Isn't that the heart of every human anyway? Desiring to be wanted and loved? And isn't that the mission of Christ Himself? To call you home to be wanted and loved and to not walk alone.

Wherever you are today is right where is best for you. Believe it or not, that job you're hating in retail will one day prepare you for your next job and the next job. This hard season will prepare you for bigger challenges to come later on, and that endurance muscle you've built will come to totally crush the small little things ahead. Where you are right now may seem like a total mountain to climb, but He knows how to get you to the top, and He knows how to train you as well. Know He loves and cares for you, and He will guide you in the best way to go. Remember Proverbs 3:5-6 when in doubt of this, "Trust in the Lord with all your heart; do not depend on your own understanding. Seek his will in all you do, and he will show you which path to take."

Prayer:

Dear Lord,

Thank You for the fact that like snowflakes, we are all uniquely made by You. Lord, we pray that as we each live out our lives that we do not fall into the pit of comparison. Just as You never healed two people in the same way, You write different stories for each of us. Let us not be tempted to believe You are not working for us just because someone else's story seems to be unfolding first. Lord, we believe that just as You say in Romans 8:28 that You are indeed working all things out for Your glory and our benefit. We praise You, oh Lord. Let us trust the path, even when it looks bleak.

In Jesus name,

Amen.

When the Ugly Duckling Grew Up

Do you recall the story of the ugly duckling from long since told nursery stories? If not, in short there was an ugly duckling. She was mocked when she wasn't ignored, and no one really got to know her true character. She then grew up into a beautiful swan, and the story ends. The issue is, the story ended without sharing how the ugly duckling never actually changed inside, even if her exterior looked different.

When I was in middle school there was a fantastic little game centered around hurting nerd. Like me. It involved boys daring other boys to ask out people like a teacher, janitor, homeless person, or me. High School was a free for all of mocking my clothes, interests, and the fact I was actually decent in school. The only time I did get attention was when they needed someone to copy homework from, or tutor them for the big test. Mind you in all of this, I am in no way complaining or playing a tiny little violin. I was a chubby middle schooler who grew into an anorexic high schooler wearing clothes from Goodwill and wide rimmed glasses a decade before it was all the rage. Braces, an introverted and shy demeanor, and issues at home didn't help much either. But I was me, through and through I was me. I spent my Friday nights reading books on English Kings and Queens, meddling with the guitar, and writing poetry. For the most part, I was happy. The sad part was I didn't allow myself to be happy, I felt there something wrong with me and I hated myself. I didn't know how to fix myself, so I was honestly really cruel to myself. I starved myself endlessly and became a total bag of bones.

Senior year came to a close along with a full scholarship, contacts, no braces, and clothes from Aeropostale. My friend, Leah, taught me how to do my makeup and for the first time, I was becoming that swan. Ironically, the most popular boy in school complimented me.... on the last day of school. The years that followed were nothing short of confusing for me. I thought any invitation out was a cruel joke, and even more alarming I found that the same kind of girls that once mocked me for how I looked, now hated me for being pretty.

I was still the history loving nerd within, even if my face changed. That is where the Ugly Duckling fails, it never tells what happened afterwards. Years passed and truly by the grace of God I found my worth in Him, I found my identity in Him, and I found myself in Him. No longer is my worth or happiness tied up in the opinions of others, but in His opinion of me. But I would be lying if I said I still don't stand baffled when I get stares and not glares. I would be lying if I said I know how to handle attention. But I'm thankful for who I am, and moreover Whose I am.

I'm not so arrogant to think that I am a remarkable beauty, but I do realize I am not the same lonely nerd of High School, I'm just the adult lonely nerd that teaches kids History. Honestly, that I what shaped part of me wanting to teach. When I worked for the Apple Store I helped facilitate a few field trips, and one of those days was with a group of twelve-year-old girls. One little girl reminded me a lot of myself, so timid and sweet. She was being made fun of for bringing one of her Barbie dolls to the field trip by the other girls. Suddenly I was watching to see that though the girls were different, this was all still the same as from when I was twelve. So, I did something about it. I chimed in how I had a similar doll when I was their age, and how cool it was. The "cool" girls thinking I was cool (LOL) quickly changed their tune and complimented the girl instead. That situation changed me. I realized the role a teacher can play in situations such as these, and I wanted to do that. Many other things influenced my decision to teach of course, but this monumental day showed me that we adults have a wonderful duty to change the future. We can stop the cycles of bullying and unjust ridicule by our influence. It won't snuff out the fires of every bully, but it can make a difference.

With that, that's the point. No one has gone through life without a moment of bullying or hurt, whether you were the victim or the inflictor, but we can change the future. We can choose love over hate, and we can teach it to the next generation. We can raise up a generation that focuses on what we have in common over what sets us apart. We can encourage kindness over being rude. And we can love. Be the change you want to see in the world, y'all.

Prayer:

Dear Lord,

We praise You for working in our lives. We praise You that even when our lives look as if we are perpetually fixed in one place, that You are working in the background. Lord, we praise You for this, and we pray that we would not be resistant to Your inner workings in us. We praise You, oh God.

In Jesus name,

Amen.

Eating Disorders

Since the Fall of man the concept of shame has plagued human kind. In the account in Genesis it says how after Adam and Eve ate the forbidden fruit and sinned for the first time, they felt shame. They hid from God in shame of what they had done, they found coverings to cover their bodies as they felt shame for being naked, they created a separation from God and it terrified them. Thousands of years later, are their grandkids really all that different?

Shame will manifest itself in many different ways, the root of shame can be of various places. Perhaps it is a complex of not feeling loved, or being poorly loved. Perhaps it is of not feeling adequate or good enough. Perhaps it is something very deep hidden away in the crevasses of the soul that we would rather not have brought up. But shame will make people do things to themselves they wouldn't do to their worst enemy.

For some this self hatred and shame will manifest in an eating disorder, like it did with me. In my blog writings I've gone into my eating disorder at a pretty surface level. I felt so proud of say up to a month ago that I was four years clean. I went four years silencing those loud voices in my head encouraging me to hurt myself, to hate myself. But then I relapsed.

Paul encourages in Corinthians to confess to one another, and I suppose this is my confession. Not only did I relapse into my anorexic tendencies again, but I became bulimic. I made myself vomit on purpose. I say this in a very serious tone, for what I did was so wrong. I took this body, this beautiful body given to me by God Himself, an image of Himself crafted so finely to be an image bearer for Him on earth, and I treated it like trash. I shamed it for any ounce of fat, I called it ugly and less than, I deprived it from food like a prisoner. But isn't that what the enemy wants? For us to be prisoners of the mind and of him and of lies and deceit? And to make it worse, I made this body cough up food on purpose. The amount of shame I felt was overbearing. Not only this, but the fact that I stood in front of the group of eighth grade girls I lead a small group for and encouraged them that week in their own beauty and adequacy, yet I made the body I abide in feel the exact opposite. Jesus calls us to love others as ourselves, but perhaps we need to love ourselves like we love others at times too.

The main difference through this relapse that took place was that I really fully left this shame and pain at the cross. I didn't merely take it to God while still holding it in my hand, but instead I left it right there. In its full ugliness and gave it to Him. I stopped hiding it from Him just like Adam and Eve did, I let Him see it. The response was honestly the most beautiful occurrence and revealed to me more of the character of God. I felt loved. In all the shame I felt, in the condemnation I felt I deserved, and He just loved me.

As I write this letter, it is Good Friday. I am reminded of another sinner who also felt he deserved shame and punishment for not making the mark, but instead was mind blown in surprise. The thief on the cross hung next to Jesus on Calvary the day of His death, and in courage he left his shame literally at the cross, and what he found was love. Jesus told him that he would be in paradise that night with Him. This is the story of Christ, He took the shame we should carry for the sins we commit, and He washed them clean with His blood. In return, He gives us love.

To whomever is reading this, I encourage you, whatever your shame, give it to Him. Whatever holds you prisoner, whatever could be called and make you freeze in terror if anyone possibly ever knew, give it to Him. Give Him your shame, and let Him give you love in return. It is not deserved, but I don't think the point of God making us was for us to ever earn anything to deserve it. For He is a Good Father, and He gives good gifts solely because of that. Let go of the shame, hand it to Him. He will bring beauty from those ashes and the label that once was a scarlet letter on your chest will become the very thing you share that He set your free from and loved you through.

Prayer:

Dear Lord,

Thank You for healing. Thank You that you see us just as You saw the first man and woman in Your own image. Help us not to fall snare to the traps set by the enemy that we are less than or not beautiful. Help us to see ourselves and others as You see them. Lord, we praise You that You are a God that makes beautiful things, and we pray that we would not only believe that, but live that out.

In Jesus name,
Amen

Forgiveness

We've all heard the saying, "holding a grudge is like drinking poison and hoping the other person dies" but it holds a lot of truth. Not a single person on the planet can say they've never been wronged, hurt, or needed to forgive someone. The truth of the matter is, it is extremely hard to do at times. It is only natural to want to hold on to that bitterness, to hold on to that chip on our shoulders complaining that we were wronged, but what if we shoved off those chips on our shoulders and walked free? What if we actually realized that we aren't perfect or blameless either? What if we took into our guts what we have been forgiven of?

Ephesians 4:32 remarks, "Be kind to one another, tenderhearted, forgiving one another, as God in Christ forgave you." God sent His own Son to forgiveness of our sins. Relient K says it best, "the beauty of grace is that it makes life not fair," we don't deserve grace or goodness or blessings, yet Christ died for us ever still. We lie, cheat, steal, hurt others, idolize the wrong things, yet He forgave us. You may have read that list and felt exempt from committing those sins, but I bet you dollars to donuts that if you really think about it, you're guilty of one of those even today maybe. This chapter isn't to make you feel guilty, but rather to help you rejoice that you are forgiven when you take that to the cross. Being given that freedom, that debt fully paid gift, how can we not share that? How can we not forgive others as God forgave us?

Forgiveness truly is a choice, and a hard one at that. For a long time, I held on to the hurt someone I care very much for imposed on me. He hurt me, he left me to go around and around in my head of my own flaws, imperfections, and issues because he was so silent for so long. I wrote him nasty letters I stashed under a bed imposing so much guilt on him, but it was in a tearful moment of prayer with God that I realized the truth: he is a flawed human. I am sure he would never consciously want to hurt me, but even if he did, he is human. He is a flawed human just like me and we will hurt each other whether we intend to or not. We will let our flesh win out over our spirits at times, and the results will sting those we care deeply about. But just as we would hope they would forgive us, we need to forgive others.

I hope I am not sounding preachy here, and this is such a worn-out topic that I won't exhaust too many pages on the subject, but it's vital to recognize the need for forgiveness. It is vital to act upon forgiving.

There is also the aspect of forgiving yourself for things. That can almost be harder, for you have to allow yourself to be free from something you've caused or done. That weight is heavy and burdensome, at times overwhelming. Truly, taking the need to forgive yourself or others to Christ is the only way to be truly free. He can, and He will help you move forward. you just have to ask.

Prayer:

Dear Lord,

We thank You for forgiveness. We thank You that You died so that we may live, and that You did this not by our own deserving or works, but because You are a God of Love. Lord, we pray that just as You forgave us, that we would be able to forgive those who have wronged us, and ourselves. As You say in Your pray, "forgive us our sins, as we forgive those who sin against us." Lord, help us in this journey. Help us beyond our own fleshly desires to hold grudges and help us to walk into the freedom that comes from truly forgiving.

In Jesus name,
Amen.

Off the Cuff Moment

We interrupt this chapter to bring yet another "pulling a Cally." I must note that I did not indeed coin this phrase, but my ever-loving friends did. Any who, I am at the chunk of my twenties where no one really asks or cares or remembers how old you are. So, in July I was asked how old I was by some long-lost Aunt and I responded. My dear mother was in the room as well, and when we got in the car she asked me why I had responded that I was 25, for I was 24. I assured my dear mother that she was mistaken, because of the math of the year I was born (1992) to the current year.....and yeah, so I was actually 24. I had spent 7 of 12 months of my 24th year thinking I was 25....and this my friends, was "pulling a Cally" at its finest. (It should be noted that an entire year later this occurred again.)

Wake Up

More than anything, I desire this book to be as such that anyone reading it can relate or somehow absorb some of the pointers or lessons or events. This chapter is going to be a little different, for it was something I experienced alone, but I feel is something every woman of God must go through: waking up.

Now, you just read that and thought, "ummmm, but Cal, I wake up every day." This is a different kind of waking up. Let me explain,

In April of 2017 my cousin and I prayed deeply for hours for someone we cared about. That afternoon I was exhausted and decided to take a nap. During this nap, I had a dream that was very, well, unique. In the dream, I was watching myself sleep at that moment. Same green top, same room, same everything. As I watched myself sleep, then suddenly an older version of me came walking in. She was fearless, clothed in dignity and white, with flowing brown hair. She did not look down, she did not stumble. She was confident, yet humble, and she walked with pure love and kindness. She knelt down at my bedside and placed a hand upon my back, suddenly I felt the hand on my back. She whispered something to me, and with that I woke up. For months, I wrestled with what all of that meant, but more than anything I desired to become her. She was a strong woman of God who had seen His faithfulness. I imagine a bit like Hannah, the mother of Samuel, after her promise fulfilled.

God gave me the verse; Isaiah 51 and I feel it is pertinent for every woman seeking after Him. Isaiah 51 says,

> "Awake, awake, arm of the Lord,
> clothe yourself with strength!
>
> Was it not you who dried up the sea,
> the waters of the great deep,
> who made a road in the depths of the sea
> so that the redeemed might cross over?
>
> Those the Lord has rescued will return.
> They will enter Zion with singing;
> everlasting joy will crown their heads.
> Gladness and joy will overtake them,
> and sorrow and sighing will flee away.
>
> "I, even I, am he who comforts you.
> Who are you that you fear mere mortals,
> human beings who are but grass,
>
> that you forget the Lord your Maker,

who stretches out the heavens
and who lays the foundations of the earth,
that you live in constant terror every day
because of the wrath of the oppressor,
who is bent on destruction?
For where is the wrath of the oppressor?

The cowering prisoners will soon be set free;
they will not die in their dungeon,
nor will they lack bread.

For I am the Lord your God,
who stirs up the sea so that its waves roar—
the Lord Almighty is his name.

I have put my words in your mouth
and covered you with the shadow of my hand—
I who set the heavens in place,
who laid the foundations of the earth,
and who say to Zion, 'You are my people.'"

We need to wake up and see the truth here.
When we allow Him to come into our lives and

become His children, we are His. He protects His own. No longer should we sleep in our own delusions that we are unworthy, disliked, an outcast. We need to wake up into the beautiful reality beyond this world. We need to wake up into the loving arms of Him Who died to save us and make us free.

I love the imagery of verse 11 that gladness and joy will come, and we will enter into this abundance singing. This is not to say that waking up into this woman will be easy. In fact, it will be painful and hard at times. Hosea 6 says,

"He has torn us to pieces
but he will heal us;
he has injured us
but he will bind up our wounds."

In many ways, this in itself is what sanctification looks like. In order for a muscle to grow bigger and stronger, it must be torn and heal back again. That's why we find ourselves sore after a long workout, and that's why during seasons of sanctification in full force, we find ourselves feeling torn. The greater glory we must be attuned to and hold so firm to in the darkest days is that those tears will be healed and made right. Those tears will make us stronger and better. What a not coincidence too that the same spelling of, "tear" is used for something that is torn and broken *and* the wet droplets that arise from eyes from gladness and pain. It's all connected, it's all a greater metaphor of His goodness really.

So, wake up. Allow those tears to form and drop in front of Him, and be restored by Him in the right ways. Wake up into life, and life abundantly. There is perseverance to be built, which in turn makes for character, which births hope. The hope in Him. Wake up into hope, my friends.

Prayer:

Dear Lord,

Thank You for how we can count on the sun to rise each morning, and in the same way, we can count on your mercies. Lord, we pray that if we are not attuned or in touch with what You are doing in our lives, You would, "wake us up" to what You are doing. Just as Paul was blind and did not see until You opened his eyes, Lord please open our eyes. Please pour Your Spirit upon us and give us a new vision and glimpse into Your heart for us. Lord, we praise Your glorious name.

In Jesus name,

Amen.

Chapter III: Teammates

Seasonal Blooms

Bows before beaus, yeah, I know that's not the term, but I am from the South and we don't say certain things in good company. Nevertheless, it's Girl Code to put your girls before guys, but what happens if the girls you are valuing that high see a change in tide within your friendships?

Friendships are a type of relationship between humans, and because of that human aspect, they are not perfect. What is important to realize is that friendships can be given or adjusted by God for certain reasons and seasons.

Friendships are very dynamic and different than a relationship with a significant other or family member, because they do not carry a blood or vow commitment. They are mutually bound only by the weight of importance by both parties, but nothing more than that. This is why at different times you may find yourself closer to one friend and then even months later very distant from them.

Different seasons in your life will come into play with friendships, because there will be times when you're both headed in different directions. There is nothing wrong with this, but it does not always feel comfortable.

Ecclesiastes 3:1 says, "There is a time for everything, and a season for every activity under the heavens." Solomon wrote the book of Ecclesiastes and he was known as one of the wisest men to ever walk the earth, and what he said was very true. Everything has its season, including friendships. Some friendships are like flourishing olive trees that endure and sustain for a lifetime, but some are like those inexpensive flowers for 99 cents at Lowe's; they only last a short while. The beauty is that God will have bring in the olive trees at the right time, as He will the little blooms that are needed to make life a little grander for a while too. What is key is letting Him have that say, and letting Him pull weeds when necessary.

Often times we don't even realize weeds are weeds until someone points them out to us, or their true ugliness is revealed. I spend a lot of time in my garden, and from time to time I will find a weed hiding in the midst of all the flowering strawberry plants, hidden so I nearly miss it until it grows very large and creates a problem. That is a direct metaphor for some people in your life, you may not know they are a "weed" until they become a problem. More often than not, we miss seeing the weeds until they become an issue since we are on the same level as those strawberry plants. Everything looks green and golden from eye level, but God can see from overhead. If we every so often pray and let Him clean up our lives and clear out weeds, sure we will lose friends, but we can have more room to grow and there is more room for good and healthy people to come into our lives. Do not be afraid to pray out the weeds in your life, it may save you from a lot of heartache and issue.

At other times a friend may not be a weed, but God will remove them from our lives and it hurts. Even losing a friend by slowly drifting apart does not feel very comfortable. It's awkward and you find yourself wanting to text them, but write and delete it five times before giving up. We feel saddened, confused, and lost at how to handle losing a friend when there really wasn't a solid reason to lose them. They important key here is to trust God. That can never be said enough really. God knows what is up around the corner for you and for them, and it may not be the best season for your friendship to be as vibrant. It doesn't soften that pull as much as we would hope, but in time it becomes evident more often than not why those friendships saw a season of waning.

"Every good and perfect gift is from above, coming down from the Father of the heavenly lights, who does not change like shifting shadows." comes from James 1:17 and it's true in anything, God does not change, and all good things come from Him. That being said, shouldn't we trust Him with all of our earthly relationships too? It's easier said than done, but ultimately, He is the giver of all good things, so when we place those relationships in HIs hands, He will give us His best for the season.

Here's another way to look at it, but putting down and sacrificing our own selfish wills and letting Him take lead, we are offering to Him some of the most important and vital pieces of our lives. He sees that and cherishes it, not considering it to be worthless, but because of Who He is, He blesses that offering. Malachi 3:10 says, "Bring the whole tithe into the storehouse, that there may be food in my house. Test me in this," says the LORD Almighty," and see if I will not throw open the floodgates of heaven and pour out so much blessing that there will not be room enough to store it." In this case, we are offering these relationships, our time, and our will to Him. He promises that He will bless that, because as it said in James, He is never changing or failing. God cares about all the little details of your life, and the company you keep will impact your life. He cares very much about that, and in trusting Him to direct every one of those relationships, He will direct you correctly.

Communication with friends is another very important aspect of a healthy friendship. If you find that a friendship is having issues or waning, and it is not of God, simply having a deep talk may change everything. As women, we feel such a pressure to be perfect all the time and hold our chins up and feelings sucked into our gut, but much of the purpose of close girlfriends is that we can let all of that out. We can be comfortable and not have to wear the mask we put on for society. The key is, being willing to take off that mask and be vulnerable within our friendships.

Let God be the Gardener of your life, and He will create fields of blooms for every season and reason under the Son, but be open to being vulnerable as deeply rooted in those good friendships too. You never know what they might yield ahead.

Prayer:

Dear Lord,

Thank You for the seasons. Thank you that each is wonderfully different than the previous, and thank You that we are able to experience that here on this earth. While we are on this side of the Veil, it is often unknown what You have planned, but Lord we pray that we do not resist the changing seasons. We pray that just as the leaves do not fuss to change color in Autumn, we would gracefully embrace Your changes and know that they are for greater vibrancy and glory and understanding in You.

In Jesus name,
Amen

Building Your Team

Pack, gang, squad, or team; you need people who have your back.

A wise person once said, "show me your friends, and I'll show you who you are." There is such truth in that statement! The Bible has a similar way to say the same thing, "Do not be misled: "Bad company corrupts good character." (1 Corinthians

15:33). Who you choose to surround yourself with effects how you act, what you do, what your life looks like. This is why it is actually a good thing to be picky with who you invest your time with.

Investing your time is a lot like investing your money: a limited resource that can yield a good or bad return. Investing your time in people who build you up will result only well, whereas investing in people who tear you down, make you feel low will only breed demise. Ecclesiastes 4:9 says, "Two are better than one, because they have a good return for their labor: If either of them falls down, one can help the other up." This verse typically pertains to spouses, but the core of it means one person encouraging another person in Christ. There is no greater thing a friend can do than encourage someone in Christ. As you read this book, I sincerely hope you are at an upturn in your life where everything is working out well, but I can sadly promise that will not always be the case. When the world is falling apart around you, you will need a team of fellow believers to encourage you to fight the good fight, trust when there seems to be no way, and seek God in all things. A team is not merely a group of friends to enjoy life with, it's a group of friends to go through life with.

The concept of, "going through life" is a very dynamic and special. A group of friends, or a friend where venturing through ups and downs, joys and sorrows, or just events and movie nights is woven into the fabric of your life. This is what life is made up of, a million little moments connecting together into a dynamic and unique tapestry.

Going through life with friends in many ways is the day to day. It is taking a cycle class together a few times a week. Its phone calls on the drive home to spitball ideas on how to approach your boss on an issue. It is waiting in the waiting room as your close friends have their first child. It is all the little moments that add up into a life. It is nothing short of beautiful.

Just like drafting for a good sports team, building your team takes patience, practice, and prayer. Pray for good and godly people to come into your life to help you grow as a person. God will usher in people into your life at just the right time.

Matthew 7:9 says, ""Which of you, if your son asks for bread, will give him a stone? Or if he asks for a fish, will give him a snake? If you, then, though you are evil, know how to give good gifts to your children, how much more will your Father in heaven give good gifts to those who ask him!" So, ask!

Ask God to build your team, and with them build your life.

Prayer:

Dear Lord,

Thank You for friendships. Thank You for creating fellowships with one another to grow and seek Your kingdom. Lord, You said it is not good for man to be alone, and so Lord we pray that You would build and foster "teams" if You will of fellow believers with the goal of glorifying Your name above all else.

Help us to challenge each other and build one another up, always keeping the focus on You.

In Your name,

Amen.

Love Many, Trust Few

My grandmother had this little wooden sign in her house that said, "love many, trust few, and always paddle your own canoe." My mom always thought it rather abrupt, but I found it to have a lot of truth. As Christians, we are called to indeed love all, but loving someone and trusting someone are two different things entirely. I think about even my closest friendships and how deep the wound has gone if they break my trust, but in the same accord I regret in hindsight how I have let those jaded feelings of protecting my heart raise up my walls beyond the borders of trust. So, what is the right way to approach trust?

Trust is a lot like respect, it must be given and upheld, but can be hard to earn back once tainted. Trust is an animal all its own, and when broken, forgiveness must be given first before any trust rebuilt. Angela Thomas said, "When a woman has a kingdom heart, she has an active understanding of what matters most to the heart of God. She lives in the balance of passion and contentment. She learns to love well, give without regard to self, and forgive without hesitation. The woman with a kingdom heart may have a duffel bag full of possessions or enough treasures to fill a mansion, but she has learned to hold them with an open hand. Hold everything with open hands. I don't think we are ever allowed to grab hold of anything or anyone as though they matter more than the Kingdom of Heaven. When you hold relationships with open hands, then people come in and out of your life as gifts of grace to be cherished and enjoyed, not objects to be owned and manipulated. And then when you hold your dreams with open hands, you get to watch God resurrect what seemed dead and multiply what seemed small." There is so much in this quote that just grabs at me, but I think a lot of the meat here is about having open hands. Letting these relationships where we allow and build trust to first be rooted and established in love (God) and then if He pulls them out, or flourishes them, it is ok. We are ok, even if that friendship ends for a time or for good.

I think that is what trust really is rooted in, trust in God. Then trusting everyone else becomes secondary and by all means broken trust can hurt, but forgiveness can come about too. So, love many, trust few deeply, and paddle that canoe.

Prayer:

Dear Lord,

Trust is such a tricky thing to navigate. Help us know when to guard our hearts, or when to let walls down and embrace fully. Lord, You and You alone know the proper and correct methods of this with each individual circumstance, and Lord we pray for Your direction and love in this.

In Jesus name,
Amen

When a Friend Gets a Boyfriend

Like the seasons, dynamics change with time. It is a part of life, and it is a part of getting older. This is especially true when a friend gets a boyfriend, or a spouse, or a child. Each of those new normals invoke the friendship you have to change in some way, if it remains completely the same, a large portion of that person's life is being left out of your friendship with them. The question then comes up, what do you do when your friend gets a significant other and you are still single?

For starters, it is important to be supportive, it is an exciting event when a friend finds someone they click with, and it is important to let them know you support them. This is a good opportunity for you to make a good friend as well in that new person, and more often than not, good people know good people. There is a good chance too that your friend will be a little insecure in a brand-new relationship, and they will look to you for support and love during this time. Let your friendship be a safe zone where your friend can speak freely and openly, and rely that all that is said will be in confidence.

What about jealousy? It is a natural emotion to become jealous, especially if you feel like someone stole your best friend. It will not be forever that they seem to solely be occupied by their new person, they will still need a best friend. Who else is going to go with them to get their nails done? You are not being replaced, you are just growing in dynamic. One day you will have someone too and it will change and help you to understand the newness of it all, so don't let jealousy on your end ruin your friendship.

What about red flags you see? I've always said, the way I can tell if a friend has found, "the one" is that they are the very best version of themselves I've ever seen. There have been times where I've seen massive red flags in the person they've chosen, such as a controlling manner, being pulled away from God, or bad behaviors. In this case, be gentle. Be supportive of your friend, but do not always be silent. Kindly and gently present to them the concerns you have and see, but be very articulate in how you approach it. Above all else, pray for that person and the entire situation. I've actually prayed before that if the couple was not meant to be, God would break them up. If they were meant to be, God would allow my view to change to better see the good in it all. God is in control, but we must let Him drive for that path to properly take place in His timing.

When a boyfriend becomes a husband, it is a new ballgame then as well. Suddenly your friend is living with this guy of theirs, and their time is due to be spent with the spouse more than for their own choosing. Again, this is when it is important to be loving, gentle, and patient with your friend. Rejoice with them in this new season, rejoice with them that God has blessed a relationship as far as marriage, rejoice in the new freedoms and experiences they have to enjoy. One day the favor will be returned, and they will be rejoicing alongside you as well.

Prayer:

Dear Lord,

Thank You for the gift of friendship. Thank you that our friendships grow and change along with us. Help us be mature in our friendships, and above all else glorify You in them, so that we may enjoy the kinds of beautiful friendships You destined for us to have. Help us not to become jealous, anxious, or insecure, rather, let us come into the abundance of You.

In Jesus name,
Amen.

Chapter IV: School

College

College. At long last you've moved your tassel to declare your independence from High School. Everyone is asking what you're doing next, and if it requires more school, you're headed to a university and the world seems ready to be conquered by your eighteen-year-old self. You have a hidden sense of confidence that you are a full-blown adult and have achieved all you will ever need to know to be successful ahead, because after all you are legally an adult.... then comes the first day on campus.

It feels slightly like a flashback to kindergarten, where everyone is your age, but you know no one, the bigger kids are slightly intimidating, and you secretly want to hold on to your parents for dear life. It's ok, it's normal to feel this.

College in society has become almost like a rite of passage. That is not to say that college is for everyone, because it's not, but it is for many people the next step necessary for a career depending on what you would like to do next. College is an entire new world full of new possibilities and opportunities to learn more about yourself, God, and who God made you to actually be.

I remember first starting out at college. I began at Randolph-Macon College, which was not a Christian school. I honestly never wanted to go to college, but my parents had desired for me to go my entire life since they did not have the ability to do so. I worked my little 104 lb. butt off to get a scholarship, and I ended up with a full ride. Randolph Macon was not my first choice by a long shot. I had actually dreamed of going to the University of Richmond, but God had different plans. Albeit my disappointment, I sought to make the best of 'ol Randy Mac. I was not prepared, nor did I expect what I found there.

Everything I believed in was challenged and questioned the first day. The adolescent childhood of Veggie Tales and goodnight prayers was mocked and questioned as I stepped into the lion's den. Finding my own voice and questioning what I truly believed became a daily occurrence. It was easy to slip into the shadows at a school, yet a deep longing for companionship grew steadily.

We began in a class designed around changing the way one thinks. What this really meant was that the college professors sought to challenge us in what we were taught growing up to be (literal) Gospel truth. Some of the prerogatives were in good taste, an honest approach to break the social barriers of money or status. The most astounding finding was that everything in my life was now held at question. There were no black or white answer keys handed to me, it was the real world.

Something that became very evident as well was the pressure of temptation. I know, I know, this is a dime store term given to us constantly throughout our childhoods to keep us on what the church culture deems correct, but it became real. The access to alcohol or drugs was extremely easy, as was the desire to fit in.

It became evident that these kids came to party, and party they did. I remember walking down the street to find a girl literally passed out in a bed of flowers on like the third day of classes. So where does this leave us? What is the line between living the right way and going too far?

In our lives, there is a constant balance of living in the world and not living of it, which at times can feel impossible to figure out the good spot. Especially in college with all of the temptations so easily obtained, it only adds to potential for the scales to be made uneven quickly. Here are my two cents on it all:

1) Take a good hard introspective look at yourself. Who are you? What do you believe? Do you believe that because your parents told you to, or because it is truly what has been revealed and made known to you? If so, how are you going to defend it?

2) Ask questions and look for wise leaders who are doing well and have a good relationship with God, and watch them.

3) Pray about EVERYTHING!

4) Don't lose yourself trying to become someone you aren't. Together with God, figure out what is most important to you and what your end goals are as a person.

5) Don't stress about a major, it will come, and it will be made clear. Take a variety of courses early to see what you enjoy doing.

6) Take as many CLEP tests as the college will allow to throw out GenEds.

7) Join clubs and make friends of every type, don't remain in your own safe little bubble.

8) Realize those you let in your inner circle will rub off on you, so ensure your own statutes take precedence as well.

9) Spend these years discovering who you are, who God made you to be, and where you are going. Spend as much time as possible in the Word and in prayer. Not a moment of that is squandered.

10) Be open to changing plans

Prayer:

Dear Lord,

Thank You for the gift of learning. Lord, let us never become so wrapped up in the belief that education is a marker of success, but let us hold firmly that education is to be used to understand You and the world around us more. Let us do all things, including school or trade, in Your glory.

In Jesus name,
Amen.

Off the Cuff

My wildest story from college was when we were all really bored and sitting around, and I kept being annoying and playing "Friend Zone" over and

over on my guitar, so my roommate suggested we go
to Target and we bought some cookie dough and I
was such a rebel and ate it raw because my mom
would never let me do that. If I eat sugar I get really
crazy and hyper, so we started dancing around in our
dorm and stuff and then we got really thirsty, so we
went to every fast food restaurant and ordered
waters because why not? So, we ordered waters at
like 6 different places and then we saw this party bus
that hit a truck and a bunch of ricers, so we went
back. So, the moral of the story is, if you give a Cally
a cookie, she becomes crazy and will jump in the
eternal flame down at Regent for a bonfire. (Note
that literally 0 alcohol or drugs were consumed. Only
sugar and pure weirdness.)

What Success Looks Like

What is success? How do we accurately
measure something that is so arbitrary to opinion,
for success is really a measure of opinion more often
than not. If success is like beauty and in the eye of
the beholder, how then do we truly say if someone is

successful or not? What does the Bible say of
success?

Perhaps the best example of measures of
success are the parable of the talents in Matthew 25.
In the story, a master gives three people either one,
five, or ten talents. Their approaches are all different
and based on their own characters and skill sets. The
one with ten invests and comes back with twenty.
Likewise, the one with five invests and comes back
with a return as well. The last one takes a different
approach, in fear the servant with a single talent
buries his talent. When the master calls them all
back, the first two are rewarded with more talents to
go forth and do even more, but the one who chose to
bury his talent was condemned, for he wasted his
talent. This is a good measure of success. To whom
much is given, much is required. Let that sink in
again, to whom much is given, much is required. So
then what is required of us?

Micah 6:8 says, "No, O people, the Lord has told
you what is good, and this is what he requires of you:
to do what is right, to love mercy, and to walk

humbly with your God." We are all given different skills sets, different gifts, and different challenges from day one of this life. What is important is how we react, how we use the talents given. The key to realize with these talents, is that talents are not always what we would think of when it comes to gifts. At times these talents can feel burdensome, but what if we used these hard knocks in life to become the foundation of our testimonies? What if we used the hard things in life to propel us further? What if even the hard aspects of life would make us better instead of bitter?

One of the most overlooked, but amazing miracles in a healing was Bartimaeus (Mark 10). He was blind, and he came to Jesus for help. Many of the blind people Jesus had healed took their healings and walked away, in many ways they took their talents and buried them. Bartimaeus instead followed Christ all the way to Calvary. He saw the fulfillment of the promise and went forward to share the Gospel for the rest of his life. He began his life with few talents, but used his gift to make him better and not bitter. He used what he was given and produced an abundance of fruit.

Our time here on earth is short, so we should use every stitch of our time here well. How sad would a life be if it were squandered, how sad would it be if we were saved and didn't share the Good News with others?

Success in a worldly mindset is typically wealth, fame, or looks. God shows us that true success is a fruitful and deep relationship with God, and doing the work He calls us to do here on earth. That doesn't mean that fame is bad, fame or position if anything is a full ten talents, to be used for His glory and ministry more than our own selfish ambitions.

How can we put that into practice? For starters, we can be kind. We can have courage. We can stand for Christ even when it's hard. We can be kind to those who the rest of the world shuns. This can be as simple as sitting with someone at lunch no one else wants to sit with, or being kind to a homeless person on the street corner. It can mean having the courage to be kind, and to show the world what it really means to be a follower of Christ. The world has been jaded with the lie that a follower of Christ is judgmental, hard, hurtful, and hateful, and it is our duty to prove them wrong. A day lived in kindness and sharing the love of Christ is a day well lived. We can do everything in our power not to squander the time we are given. God is the only One Who knows how many days we have left, so we should use those days to their fullest. Let us not grow weary in the work, and when we do, let us come to Him for comfort. Let us know that our work, even if we cannot see the fruit, is not in vain. Let us know that the Holy Spirit is alive and at work in each of our lives all the time. Let us hold firm to these truths and let us go forward believing them, for one day (if even in Heaven) we will see the abundant harvest.

Prayer:

Dear Lord,

Thank You for the fact that success is something not measured by wealth or education, but by working each day to glorify You. Let us not grow weary if we do not see the fruit harvested on this side of the Veil that it is in vain, rather, let us hold firmly to the knowledge that You see all and know all, and that all will work for the glory of You in the end. Use us, oh Lord, use us well so that we may hear one day, "well done My good and faithful servant."

In Jesus name,

Amen

What They Don't Teach You In School

I am a teacher, and with the title comes some pretty rad revelations. It's so strange being on the other side now of the classroom, it's a lot like being a bird. You get to see everything from overhead, but now they can't bully you and call you names to your face. Somehow, I ended up the "cool teacher" of the school, but I think that is because they have no earthly idea how nerdy I actually am deep down. Nevertheless, there are many aspects of school that are lacking in the education system in America today. Sure, it is great to learn about the Civil War or the components of a cell, but what about character? What about taxes? What about how to finance a car loan with no credit history? There is a lot that they don't teach in school, but they really should. I won't spend the rest of this chapter going on and on about how to do your taxes, but I will offer a few tips of advice as the teacher I am. So, enjoy. Then, class is dismissed until the next chapter when we really get to what you want to know about.... boys.

1) Establishing credit is hard, but then it's easy too. Store cards are a great way to establish credit for the first time, as are student offered cards. Establishing credit early will help you down the road for things like car loans or even buying a house.

2) Taking more deductions will get you more money monthly, rather than the large sum after tax returns. It's really more of if you're smarter with a large amount of cash or piece meal, but either way plan to tithe at least 10% and then save 50%.

3) Sewing is a basic skill that few people master, but it comes in such handy. From fixing buttons, mending clothes, or even making dresses it can save you time and money. If you're short like me, it will save you a bundle in tailoring as well.

4) Live at home as long as possible, but SAVE SAVE SAVE. Plan for the future and stash up those stacks

5) Learn to change your own oil, rotate tires, and inflate tires. You never know if you'll be stuck in Minnesota at midnight in 12-degree weather with a flat tire and need to know how to inflate it back up again.

6) Be wise with purchases, but don't forget to have a little fun once in a while too. Buy the shoes.

7) Have a solid resume. Listen to TED talks or podcasts of successful people and watch them. Watch everything and absorb.

8) Never take advice to heart from someone who is living in sin or is doing worse off than you.

9) Know when to speak and when to listen. When it comes down to it, listen far more than you speak.

10) Let kindness and courage lead you in every decision you make.

Prayer:

Dear Lord,

Please grow us in the knowledge and truths of You. Let us grow wiser through experiences and revelations, but also through observing others around us. Dear Lord, abide in us.

In Jesus name,
Amen.

Chapter V: Dating

To Quote Charlie Brown, "I Got a Rock"

Today sifting through the mail was yet another wedding announcement. This time for the younger sibling for a friend. So not only are all my friends married off or with children now, but it seems their younger siblings are beating me to the sacred alter. It can be easy to become bitter. It can be easy to fall into the mentality that there is something wrong with you, or that you are infected with some sort of plague.

Singleness really has become the modern-day equivalent to leprosy, hasn't it? Your married friends avoid inviting you to things, so you won't, "feel out of place at a couple's event" or well-meaning relatives ask if you've tried the remedy that at times yields results for some users of Christian Mingle. But what if it isn't that there is something wrong with you, rather God is just not finished working on you? That you're holding out for the best person God has for you, and along the way He is developing you as well? What if it's not that we are being patient and waiting on God, but He's waiting on us to just let down these strongholds and trust Him?

The unfortunate downside to the beauty of things is they are rarely all that spectacular while they're being made or refined. How often do we look at a pile of dirt and find it lackluster while just below the surface the buds of a flower are forming to burst forth. The same can be said of us. Of us, of people, of the seasons of refinement when the work being accomplished in us feels anything but beautiful.

It says in Matthew 7 the parable of the snake and the stone. It highlights to earthly fathers, as human as they are, if their son would come to them and ask for some bread, he wouldn't hand him a stone or a snake. So then, how much more will your Heavenly Father do when you ask Him? For me I saw this verse and something about it struck a chord. I myself have felt stuck in a season of perpetual waiting. Not just mere waiting, but refinement and pruning (think a waiting room in Hell where your name is never called, but rather you're set on fire every day and Taylor Swift is on repeat playing).

Well. Perhaps I am being a bit overdramatic, but at times it has felt like Hell.

During this time, as well during my Bible readings God constantly would take me to every darn time in the Bible He said, "the stone the builders rejected shall become the cornerstone." Of course, I knew that meant Jesus in the Bible, but what was His angle with me on that? Last time I checked I wasn't in the construction business.

I recall wailing a cry out to God one afternoon on my bed just in sobs over how lost and confused I felt. I had done every single thing He had called for, asked, I strived to be so perfect, yet nothing seemed to change. It just got worse. I begged for this bread, I reminded Him of Matthew 5. Instead of the flood of manna I expected to fall from the sky, it was hail storm after hail storm. I felt pelted by rocks left and right. But it was with this overabundance of rock that the foundation was laid of what would one day become a massive testimony of my life. Rather, it was the rock I was given, the rock I didn't want. The rock I rejected of patience, courage, tears, and learning my own strength that would become the cornerstone of a testimony He was building. He built my life on this rock.

He knew a bread foundation wouldn't last. It would be a piece of cake, but it would fall apart and soon be forgotten. The foundation of bread would grow stale and I would grow to take it for granted.

Rather, a foundation made of stone would last forever. The garden that would grow through these rocks would need deep roots that could only be indwelled in the Richness of God Himself as He speaks of in the Parable of the Four Soils. This gift of a stone instead of bread was just that: a gift.

We may not see it until it is finished or near completion, but one day the instruments handed to us and rejected at first by our human hearts may just be the very thing that defines us.

I'd like to think myself a formidable woman of God, a fortress against these roaring waves as the Son shines down and I stand strong...but I am not. Oh, sure I have my days, days where I dismiss fear and it's shrills of lies, but this past weekend was not

one of those days. We seldom recognize that we live
in a world at war. Not merely a war between man, but
a war unseen by human eyes of good and evil. My
views of this were not widely opened until reading,
"Screw Tape Letters" in high school by CS Lewis.
Lewis vividly brings to view the behind the scenes of
the underworld and the little discreet buttons pushed
in everyone one of us to knock us down. For me
anxiety and depression are enduring thorns in my
side that are at times pushed in hard enough to make
me bleed. Paul describes in 2 Corinthians 12 of his
thorn, "I must go on boasting. Although there is
nothing to be gained, I will go on to visions and
revelations from the Lord. I know a man in Christ
who fourteen years ago was caught up to the third
heaven. Whether it was in the body or out of the body
I do not know—God knows. And I know that this
man—whether in the body or apart from the body I
do not know, but God knows— was caught up to
paradise and heard inexpressible things, things that
no one is permitted to tell. I will boast about a man
like that, but I will not boast about myself, except
about my weaknesses. Even if I should choose to
boast, I would not be a fool, because I would be

speaking the truth. But I refrain, so no one will think more of me than is warranted by what I do or say, or because of these surpassingly great revelations. Therefore, in order to keep me from becoming conceited, I was given a thorn in my flesh, a messenger of Satan, to torment me. Three times I pleaded with the Lord to take it away from me. But he said to me, "My grace is sufficient for you, for my power is made perfect in weakness." Therefore, I will boast all the more gladly about my weaknesses, so that Christ's power may rest on me. That is why, for Christ's sake, I delight in weaknesses, in insults, in hardships, in persecutions, in difficulties. For when I am weak, then I am strong."

Paul was a mighty man of Christ, gifted with glimpses of the future, of Heaven, of things that can only be gifted of God. As much as we think of the Bible in terms of being two thousand years ago, we must realize that the men and women in the Bible were exactly as us-human. They were like many of us and humans called to a greater purpose than the mundane lives we aspire to and into a service for God. This service will yield no greater joy than Christ

Himself, but no greater opposition than the enemy against God in every act.

I have been through such seasons of boot camp of sanctification and growth in the Lord, and I acquiesce that that times I have become a tad prideful in how far I've come in this journey that I neglect to recall the most vital thing of all: I am not enough, and God is. Over a weekend I came to the end of myself, the end of my own strength, the end of my own understanding and controls and cried out to Jesus begging Him to come and surround me in His grace. I begged to hear His voice or to be given a comforting verse in His Word. In my own lacking, He surrounded me with His love and made up for my lacking abundantly more than all I could ask for or imagine. I do not believe God causes storms in our lives, but I do believe He allows for the thorns to endure at times, so we see our desperate need for Him.

At the end of ourselves we find the void, and the only thing that can fill that void is Christ Himself.

Prayer:

Dear Lord,

Thank You that we know that even when it does not make sense, that You are working to grow us and fill us with You. We praise and extol You, oh Lord.

In Jesus name,
Amen

The Desire to have a Boyfriend

One of the most marking traits of high school is who is dating whom. It is an inescapable fact of life that during early high school the little alarms within our bodies seem to ring loudly, blaring, and in direct sight someone who you paid no mind to the day before suddenly becomes surrounded by a choir of angels when they smile.

More often than not, high school relationships start and end as fast as interest in a second period science class.

There are instances where high school relationships actually pan out to being something more. John Ragan and Kelly Dunner began dating in the 10th grade. It ended up being the spectacle of the year when they broke up at the science fair, but later ended up back together. They dated all through college and got married the week after graduation.

The key to remember though, is 99% of high school relationships do *not* actually result in a marriage. Out of everyone in my high school, the girl that I respected most was named Maddie. Maddie had a rule to herself that she would not date until college. This was not because she wasn't sought after, not popular, not very much desired, but rather because she had the maturity to know she needed to mature into her own self before trying to form a relationship with someone else. The real question boils down to this: how can you share a relationship with someone else if you don't really know who you are?

It can be said that we spend our entire lives finding out who we truly are, and that is true that our lives are a journey into becoming who we truly are, but it is pertinent to have an understanding of your own personal goals, desires, and hopes before joining forces with another. More often than not, those aspirations will be what brings a couple together. This is often evident with ministry; countless couples will have the same calling from God for a place or cause leading to a partnership build on God and commonality.

In truth, the sole way to find your identity is to find it through Christ. CS Lewis articulately said, ""Your real, new self (which is Christ's and also yours, and yours just because it is His) will not come as long as you are looking for it. It will come when you are looking for Him. Does that sound strange? The same principle holds, you know, for more everyday matters. Even in social life, you will never make a good impression on other people until you stop thinking about what sort of impression you are making. Even in literature and art, no man who bothers about originality will ever be original whereas if you simply try to tell the truth (without caring two pence how often it has been told before) you will, nine times out of ten, become original without ever having noticed it. The principle runs through all life from top to bottom, Give up yourself, and you will find your real self. Lose your life and you will save it. Submit to death, death of your ambitions and favorite wishes every day and death of your whole body in the end submit with every fiber of your being, and you will find eternal life. Keep back nothing. Nothing that you have not given away will be really yours. Nothing in you that has not died will ever be raised from the dead. Look for yourself, and you will find in the long run only hatred, loneliness, despair, rage, ruin, and decay. But look for Christ and you will find Him, and with Him everything else thrown in." What truth is found in this! In seeking Him, we find not only Him, but our true selves.

Think about it this way, if you purchase a car and it runs for years, but then it has an issue, what do you do? Will the problem be best solved by trying to figure it out yourself, or going to the maker of the car to ask how the car works best? How to fix the issues with the car? Trying it yourself will more than likely result in being covered in muck, frustrated, and more confused than ever. The Maker knows how your wired, He knows you so much better than you know yourself, and in seeking His help, He will know what is best.

The journey to finding yourself will lead you to God, and you may even go in with an entire slew of desires and aspirations all to find that in the end, He knew better. Trust the Maker, trust the journey, trust the results will be worthwhile.

Prayer:

Dear Lord,

We praise Your Holy name. Lord, let us recognize that You are the giver of all good things, and that every good and perfect gift is from above. Let us be women of open palms, ready to hold or release whatever You would call without pushback. Lord, satisfy our hearts in You, and prepare us for what You have planned ahead.

In Jesus name, Amen.

Off the Cuff

I lost my car today. In Minnesota. In a Minnesota winter. For 30 minutes.

So, I got pretty cold. Looked pretty dumb.

Pretty sure if there were like a reality show of my life, there would be a solid 15 mins of every episode of me looking for my car.

The First Date:

Goodness first dates are exhilarating and fun. Everything is so new. Metaphorically you are standing at the threshold of a new door about to walk in and experience something you have not known before. Now, of course some first dates are going to be total duds. The kind you sort of regret, and wish you had spent watching reruns of The Office at home. Then some first dates are, well, the kind that leave you humming after you get home with rosy cheeks and that kind of smile where you bite your lower lip just a little and I swear the colors are just a little more vibrant than they were before. But let us not get to ahead of ourselves here.

You've responded, "yes" to this potential date, you've spent an hour on your hair and the majority of the day thinking through what you have in your closet and if you really need that new pair of heels and you're ready to go. You nervously wring your hands a bit, and gosh everything is happening in such a slow motion. You question back and forth if you should bring up different topics, or what you should hold back.

Here are a few tips that I've learned over the years....

1) Be yourself, you aren't a dime a dozen girl and it's important to show that you are unique. You aren't like the other fish in the sea, you are a mermaid.

2) Try to avoid topics such as politics or controversial ideas that could stir more of a debate, debating isn't a great way to start a relationship.

3) If you have a good sense of humor, let that show.

4) Don't wear clothes that are too revealing, but do show you're a lady. Tight enough to show you've a woman, but loose enough that you're a lady. Wear what you feel confident in especially.

5) If you have a nerdy side, guys love that. Star Wars, Lord of the Rings, or video games are always a good thing to show off some.

6) Always have gum and lipstick ready for a refresh.

7) Be genuine and real, don't act fake or tell a single lie. Be honest and true to yourself and God above all else.

8) If you feel uncomfortable, don't suffer through the date or feel obligated to give a second one.

9) Ask them about themselves, guys love talking about themselves and you'll learn more about them that way too.

10) Don't order anything that requires you to be messy like ribs or pasta.

11) Listen more than you speak, observe more than you convey.

12) Don't hide the fact that you are a Christian, but don't shove it down their throats either.

13) Playing with your hair makes guys crazy, I have no idea why, but it just does. Twirling it or gently flipping it will drive them mad.

14) The majority of guys do enjoy talking about cars, the outdoors, or sports so if you happen to enjoy any of those things too, don't shy away from showing that you're a tomboy. Tomboys rock.

15) Don't kiss on the first date. Cheek kisses are alright, but hold off on the big first kiss a little. Maybe date 2.

Prayer:
Dear Lord,

We give to You our dating lives, we know that dating is for the intention of marriage, and we leave it in Your hands not to be manipulated or misused.

In Jesus name,
Amen.

So, I Tried a Dating App....

The world is changing rapidly every day, so much so that even that phrase has become mundane and a tad cliché, yet it holds truth. We live in a culture where with the stroke of a few swipes, we can select a new pair of shoes off a site, or a potential date within moments. With that being said, how can we pull upon morals, depth, and integrity when it is so easy?

In truth, I knew very little about the culture of dating apps before this past week. I knew my cousin met his fiancé on one of them, and I knew a few friends who tried at them and felt frustrated, but I did not know enough to form an opinion about them.

That being said, I did some field research on the subject. That's right, I signed up for a dating app.

I chose Bagel Meets Coffee since I had a friend who had pretty good success from that one, and I fully disclosed on my profile that I was looking to interview someone, not to date them. That being said, I had very few takers after they knew what my aim was. To my pleasant surprise, I had coffee with a wonderful guy named Jeremy. Jeremy was a wealth of knowledge on the culture of the dating app from everything from good apps to use to red flags.

Like many of us, Jeremy was first intrigued by dating apps because he knew of others who had success from them. He shared that sites such as match.com and E-harmony went more in depth, and certainly seemed to have more serious clients. He felt frustrated trying to meet someone beyond work and the lackluster bar scene, so he gave the apps a shot.

On average about two weeks of chatting would happen before an actual date, which gave enough time to chat with someone and recognize any red flags before meeting the person in real life. With so many apps, many of the same people circle around the realm of the app dating world, so it was not rare to see the same person on many apps.

There were many valid pros and cons to the dating apps including:

Pro: Ease of access, up front knowledge of aspects such as beliefs, knowledge of intentions early on, avoid the bar scene, and you know they're single!

Cons: Too many options at times, easy to fall into a superficial way about things, the non-serious people clogging the pipes for those serious, and bursts of talking to many people at once can get confusing.

Overall, I am not going to give a solid opinion for or against dating apps, because at the root of it, it's the same deal as meeting someone at a cookout or wedding. There are risks involved no matter how you meet someone, and the pitfall of superficiality is prevalent no matter what. What is vital is to hold firm to your own sets of beliefs. Whether you subscribe to apps such as Bumble, Coffee Meets Bagels, or Match, you must go in with the intent of staying true to who you are. We live in a very superficial world, but at the core of it there is that human element desiring something more of substance.

At the end of my own exploration of a few of these apps, I honestly felt exhausted and a tad introspective of my own qualities, but that's where being rooted in your own skin comes to play a major role as well.

Jeremy was a delight to meet and have a coffee with, and it was certainly great to better understand such a different culture than I myself am attuned with, but all rests within the user themselves. Pray with intention and perhaps this would be the vessel in which God would bring someone into your life to date, or perhaps He has a wonderful happenstance planned elsewhere. Regardless, stay grounded, don't let looks or someone's photogenic qualities win out over substance, and go in with intention. Know that

God is very mysterious in how He works, and if you feel led, a dating app perhaps may indeed be the vessel in which God brings two souls together.

In an ever-changing world, it is good to serve a God Who never changes. He is the constant in all the change this world sees, so pray hard and be open to what He may do.

Prayer:

Dear Lord,
Guide us in our journeys and how we may go about meeting those who should be in our lives. Lord, write us love stories beyond compare, and make them beautiful just as the story of Your love for Your bride, the Church, is beautiful.
In Jesus name,
Amen.

It's Not in Vain

Being single honestly at times feels like some sort of punishment. If you're like me, you will see all your friends get married and start families before you ever have your first kiss. But I promise you this, it is not in vain unless you make it in vain.

The years between 18-35 can be your most selfish. You have the most freedom in career, relationships, and life. You are your best looking (unless you're George Clooney) during those years, and more than likely have the most opportunity to chase your own desires, dreams, and ambitions. But what if instead of living those years for yourself, you gave them to God?

In a society where the idiom, "the world is your oyster" we give few pearls to Christ. I am not saying you should go check into the nearest nunnery for these years, but what if you really handed them over to God? What if we let Him take the driver's seat, and we just trusted that He will take us to a place where we are truly happy. Oh, and along the way, we get to know the Driver all the more better.

It's a lot like a car (going to go with a car theme for this chapter for no reason at all). Shouldn't you trust the One Who made the car, rather than trying your own hand at it? That is the same in our lives. We think we know exactly what we want, how we should go about it, and what is best. The truth is, we don't. The truth is that often it doesn't seem kind or good what God will lead us through, but it defines who we are more often than not. In nearly every instance we are given the choice to become cold and hardhearted, or grow and see it as something to change us for the better.

In these years many of you will be single. Many of you will have to choose between taking the guy you know with no shadow of doubt is danger and a bad idea, and telling him yes or no. You will have opportunities to make choices that will alter your choice. You may also have times where you ask God which way to go, and He is silent. That is when you have to trust your instincts. Trust what you know of God. Trust what you have read in Scripture. Trust that He is there.

I used to look bitterly towards God for as long as He kept me single. I used to hold so much contempt towards God and my husband for how long I had to wait for my mate. I cried countless tears and begged and bargained and looked up to see nothing. Then God changed my perspective. I asked God to open my eyes after reading a story in 2 Kings 6 about Elisha, who only saw the problem, but when God opened his eyes, saw the solution: that God had it all covered. God helped me to realize that in these past few years He has grown my relationship with Him to be something so much stronger and enduring than I could have ever imagined. He has helped me to grow in maturity and in myself, so that I know with no shadow of doubt that I truly know who I am. God helped me learn to receive love, and all the pitfalls I had within myself not knowing how to receive love or to be loved. He helped me publish books and start jobs and find my calling. Sure, I dated some losers (coming up in other chapters) but He used that too. He used my mistakes to be markers of His grace. One of my favorite quotes is, "if you think you've blown God's plan for your life, rest in this: you, my beautiful friend, are not that powerful." -Lisa Bever. He uses the bad for good too.

It is a sacrifice to God to take this time and hand it over to Him. It is a sacrifice to deny ourselves of worldly desires and trust and follow Him, even when it does not make sense. But God sees those sacrifices, He sees when we choose Him over our flesh. He does not turn a blind eye or shrug it off, it matters. I for one truly believe those sacrifices come back to us as blessings. For we not only have to suffer the consequences of poor choices, but we are grown deeper into trusting Him to give us better than what the world has to offer. We come to a deeper knowledge of Who He is, and who we are in Him. We come to see that this world and this time are all so fleeting. Suddenly the old and melancholic King Solomon does not sound so morbidly depressing in Ecclesiastes, rather wise. For he knew that God was worth more than anything this world can offer. God does not scoff at our sacrifices, nor does He turn away anyone earnestly seeking His face.

When it comes to relationships, we can go based on our own selves, or we can look to Him. In my humble opinion, it is best to let Him direct everything. He made you, so He is the Only One Who knows truly who is best to fit with you. He knows who your best teammate is, He knows who He thought of when He made you, and likewise how you were thought of in the creation of the other person. Ecclesiastes 4 says that it is not good for man to be alone, two are better than one and a chord made of three (God, you, & husband) is not easily broken. Why would you ever want to settle for anyone less than who God specifically crafted for you?

This is my challenge to you: ask. Seek. Pray.

Ask God to direct your heart every time. Keep your eyes so completely focused on Him, that only through His lenses could you ever see the one He made for you. Pray against temptations. Pray for every crush you have that if it is God's will that it remains, it will, but if not, it will be snatched quicker than you can begin to start doodling his name. Pray constantly and pray for your spouse. You cannot pray for someone too much.

Sacrifice those years to God as an offering, let Him direct the path, I promise He has a plan and He will not fail. Even if it looks dark right now, keep walking in the Light. It will be worth it in the end.

Prayer:

Dear Lord,

Let us recall the reminder that our efforts are not in vain. Let us hold firm to the knowledge that You are indeed ever working in our hearts to purify and grow us into the women that You destined us to be. Let our hearts be flesh and not stone, and able to be molded to Your liking and for Your glory.

In Jesus name,
Amen.

Charlotte's Prayer on Boys

In the course of a lifetime you may be blessed enough to come across a hand full of godly women with the right perspective on life, for me one of those women is my best friend, Charlotte. Charlotte has been a part of my life since we were children, since we met in High School. Over the course of nearly a decade of friendship we both have seen our fair share of suitors and looters. Charlotte exhibits every trait a Proverbs 31 woman attains, most especially when it comes to the opposite sex.

Especially when you are younger it is so easy to fall into the mindset of "be young and free," but that freedom comes at a cost. This is not to say that marriage should be the central focus when it comes to every fleeting crush or blushing encounter, but it is vital to allow God to hold your precious heart. Your heart is the most precious gift you hold in your hands, and placed in the wrong hands it can be severely broken or manipulated. It is such a human condition, and really the root of the first sin, that somehow, we know better than the Creator Himself, but the fact is we do not. Psalm 139 shares, "My frame was not hidden from You when I was made in the secret place. When I was woven together in the depths of the earth, Your eyes saw my unformed body. All the days ordained for me were written in Your book before one came to be."

Before we were even woven together God saw every single aspect of our lives, therefore it would be completely ignorant to think somehow, we know better than Him. Yet in our own flesh and rebellion more often than not we believe we do somehow know better. The beauty of the truth of Christ is that no matter how deep we find ourselves in a mess, He is still there to help pick up back up. This all being said, we can certainly save a lot of mess and tears in trusting His hand to guide us.

Where does this leave us when it comes to guys? What are we to ask or do? Charlotte, the one I mentioned above, along the way discovered truly one of the best prayers one can ever pray; asking God to change her heart. Jeremiah 6:16 shares, "Stand at the crossroads and look; ask for the ancient paths, ask where the good way is, and walk in it, and you will and rest for your souls." What this verse is compelling the listener to do is to ask God. Charlotte had a rule that if she found herself beginning to have

feelings for a guy, she would take it to God first. She
would sacrifice her own headstrong feelings and in
sincerity as God to guide the feelings. If the feelings
were to persist, she knew it was of Him, but if they
dissipated, that was of Him as well. I cannot tell you
time after time how she was spared from some bad
guys from this simple surrendering prayer.

That leads the concept of sacrificing for the
Lord. What is sacrifice? Sacrifice is placing
something completely precious upon the alter of God
for His use. In ancient times this typically meant a
lamb or dove, but we no longer live in times where
that is necessary, for through the death of Christ on
the cross it is finished, and the curtains are torn
between God and us. Today we too can sacrifice to
Him, but with our hearts. We can place our hearts at
the throne of God most holy, give Him the most
sacred and unique possession we obtain, and trust
Him radically to give us His best. This may bring us
to a time of loneliness, this may lead us to a time of
hard-core sanctification, but it is worth it completely.
For God knows us so well that He knows what works
and what is pernicious to our very souls. Trusting

Him with such a relationship will only lead to the ultimate best choice for your love life.

Prayer:

Dear Lord,

Thank You for Charlottes's great reminder that we should place all things before Your throne for proper placement. Let us not cling so tightly to what we see easily accessible, but let us submit our hearts to You and delight ourselves in You as Psalm 37:4 says, and only then will You mold our hearts to give us the desire of our hearts. Let our greatest desire always be You, in sincerity.

In Jesus name,
Amen.

What is too Far?
Boundaries.

In a world where everything seems to go, where do we draw lines? How far is too far, when the world says, "all the way" is A-Okay?

If we are to dive into the scriptures about this subject, we have no better resource than Song of Solomon. Song of Solomon is a book in the Bible written by King Solomon himself about his dating and marriage to his wife. The entire book is centered around God, a man, and a woman, and the journey from dating to marriage. It's of utmost value, for it is the only complete book on the subject of marriage at all, and something we can draw upon when we are questioning what is right and wrong physically.

Something important to know is that sex is not sinful...inside marriage. Sex was designed by God for a husband and a wife to do, it actually is the second command God gives Adam and Eve in the Garden. He tells them to first and foremost have no other gods but Him, and then to go fill the earth (nice way of saying to just do it #Nike). God even designed both the male and female bodies to not just perform sex to make children, but to have pleasure from the act. What cannot be stressed enough is that sex is only for marriage.

Song of Solomon puts it this way, "Promise me, O women of Jerusalem, by the gazelles and wild deer, not to awaken love until the time is right." (Song of Solomon 2:7). What is beautiful here is that as women we are viewed as precious gazelles; beautiful, strong, free, and innocent. God is imploring us to not "awaken" love until the time is right in the context of marriage. Countless opinions outside of the Bible will suggest that "being in love" is good enough, but it is not. That commitment and promise of marriage is Holy. The word, "holy" literally means, "set apart, sacred" and sex is a holy act. Sex should be viewed as such, as something so beautiful and holy that it is very much worth the wait.

Elisabeth Elliot puts it this way, "The bicycle given for Christmas will not be prized like the bicycle bought with the money earned by delivering newspapers for two or three years." What she is getting at is that it will be better because there will be more anticipation, more hype, more excitement because you waited. Just like waiting for Christmas morning for presents, it will be a million times better.

Another aspect of everything comes with everything-but-sex being alright, but that is not the case either. Albeit in person I am a very discreet person, I feel it necessary to dive in if you will on such matters-because they do matter. The Bible does not give complete guidelines for all the aspects of being physical, but it does hint at quite a few.

Kissing is fine and dandy, Solomon and his bride kissed before marriage and it honestly is quite sweet. The key to remember here is that at times kissing can quickly become out of hand and reach making out and that can lead to hands where they probably shouldn't be. Solomon does not address this, but in the sense of not "awakening love" it is probably best not to rev the engines while in park.

Outside of marriage, oral sex is <u>not</u> ok. Everyone has a different opinion on the subject even within marriage, but John Piper speaks on it well, "Oral sex is even more intimate and delicate, it seems, than copulation. And we know this because even married couples are wondering if they should go there. It is as if it is a stage of intimacy that may not even be proper for married people. And to think it can be an innocent substitute for copulation so people can obey the letter of the law outside marriage is a mirage. That is the first observation." He goes on to say that within marriage, it is only right if both parties feel it is kind and comfortable. Of course, this book will not go any deeper than that, but the next book will. This book is just to set the record straight that oral sex is not ok outside of marriage. It isn't some loophole on the virgin scale, it is too far.

Boundaries are also something that you must set on your own. Some people may only feel comfortable holding hands for a very long time, and not want to cross any lines before marriage-and that is perfectly fine. If you think about it this way, if you truly love the person, you will wait. More than that, the amount of time you will have married will be so much longer than this time of dating and engagement, that you will have total freedom then, so enjoy this time right now. Enjoy the anticipation and the excitement, enjoy the Christmas Eve if you will before the big Christmas Morning.

Also, make that first kiss something special. Believe it or not, I am right now nearly twenty-five years old and have never been intimate. I've had the opportunity quite a few times, but I wanted it to be with someone I really cared for. I didn't want to just waste it to get it over with, but rather save it to be a wonderful present. I want that to be something wonderfully precious I can give. In my marriage, I want to give all of me, and I just truly feel it would be something beautiful to give only my husband such a precious gift.

This chapter was meant to be short and a mini discussion, for the next book will go far more in depth, but it is vital to talk about. It is vital to have a good and clear mindset before even a first date, because love can make you a little crazy.

Prayer:

Dear Lord,

Thank You for the gracious gifts of connecting with another person. Thank You for the good and perfect gift indeed of physical and emotional purity that can one day be given in complete love to someone else. Lord, help us know the correct boundaries in all things, and to trust Your leading and guiding hand with all such things. Help us know that it is indeed worth the wait, and that at the end there is so much glory for You and immense blessings waiting for us and our steadfastness.

In Jesus name,
Amen

Allissa's Story

Love is patient, love is kind. It does not envy, it does not boast, it is not proud. It does not dishonor others, it is not self-seeking, it is not easily angered, it keeps no record of wrongs. Love does not delight in evil but rejoices with the truth. It always protects, always trusts, always hopes, always perseveres. - 1 Corinthians 13:4-7

Growing up I had always thought of my knight and shining armor who would come rescue me and sweep me off my feet. Little did I know that the knight would be a tall, nerdy boy who would one day wear a lab coat.

In the Spring of 2013 I met Tyler. A bad country boy who always knew how to cheer me up. I fell for him. I wanted him. But he didn't want me. He didn't know Christ, so why in the world should I be with him? But I couldn't let go. I dated multiple boys, but I was always pulled back toward him. In the five years that I was in love with him, I had seen him in person a total of four times. Four times. He lived 15 minutes away from me. Yet I couldn't let him go. In the Spring of 2017 he finally told me he wanted to give this a shot. But I felt sick to my stomach. I knew this wasn't right, yet I have been waiting for how long for him to give me a chance? So I said yes. I leaped. And I fell. He used me for sexual things. He didn't want me for the person I was, he wanted me, so that I could make him feel good.

I went to Cally and told her that I had dropped him. She understood my pain, my heartache. How I was so in love, a fleshy love not a spiritual love, that I was at rock bottom. Her response was "I know it hurts now, but I promise this will result in Ephesians 3:20." "Now to him who is able to do immeasurably more than all we ask or imagine, according to his power that is at work within us. - Ephesians 3:20 Shortly after I cut ties off with Tyler, I had a summer job lined up at a Christian bible camp. Trout Lake Camps, in northern Minnesota. She kept reminding me that in God's timing he would bless me countlessly. I had a hard time believing this whole heartily, I was so torn over Tyler. So, I went up to camp for the summer. My routine was set in place, every morning I had a cabin leader meeting, I hung out with campers and I showed them the Lord's love. Pretty fun, right? I was going on my third out of eight weeks at camp and I was loving it.

So, one morning my alarm goes off, I get up and get ready for the day. I go down into where my meeting was about half an hour early because I really liked a certain couch. I walked in, plopped down on the couch and closed my eyes. I felt like someone else was in there, so I opened my eyes and there he was. Balancing on a piece of wood on top of PVC pipe, was this tall, brown haired, blue eyed cabin leader. "Hi, I'm Allen." His voice was so deep. "Hi I'm Allissa." Right off the bat I was intrigued. His smile was enough to make you weak in the knees. Before I knew it, I was looking for him around camp. Every time I would see him I would blush, smile and run away like I was twelve for unknown apparent reason. I only saw him a few times a day, but he never left my mind.

I was really struggling with if I should make the first move or not. So, I did what my instincts told me to do about it, I took it to God. I was sitting at the boat docks praying that the Lord would give me a sign. Help me know if I should pursue this Allen or if I am just looking to get over Tyler. And then it happened.

A bird pooped on me. Of all things that could have
happened, I get pooped on. Some of you might take
that as a bad sign, but I myself took it as a good sign.
Allen was a volunteer cabin leader, so he was leaving
after this week. I had multiple opportunities to ask
him for his phone number before had, but I was
literally at my last shot. He was turning in his stuff to
leave. "Hey Allen, are you here next week?" Little
secret between you and I, I knew that he wasn't, but I
needed a reason to talk to him. He proceeded to tell
me he wasn't, and we talked about our week and our
campers. I finally built up enough nerve and asked if
he wanted to exchange numbers. So, we started
texting. A lot. I mean all the time. We did the
awkward flirting like you did when you were twelve
years old. We talked about everything under the sun,
our hopes and dreams, our fears, our pet peeves. He
asked me what my favorite snack was, favorite color,
favorite animal and any other question he could
think of to keep the conversation going. I could talk
to him for hours. He told me he was coming up for
one more week, which was also the week of my 18th
birthday. I was so excited. We had all these things
planned. Canoeing during our off time, hanging out in

the sun but it was all put on halt when we were split up. Unfortunately, we didn't have the same schedule, I was with the primary kids and he was with the junior kids. We had one meeting together from 9am-9:30 but other than that we didn't have time together. Until we decided to meet at a dock at 2pm every day. Those awkward conversations on the dock made time stop. I felt like I could tell him anything. Before I knew it, I wanted Allen. I knew there was something about him that I couldn't let go. I could see Jesus reflecting off of him. He was so loving, so caring and genuine that I couldn't help but be attracted to him. I asked him one day what we were. If we were friends or more than friends. We talked about the fact I was going to college in the Fall and he was going back to school too. We didn't know if we could handle it. Allen didn't say much other than texting me that he had a serious question to ask me the next day at the dock we met at. That was also my 18th birthday.

The next morning, I woke up and was walking up the hill at camp. He was the first person to wish me a happy birthday. My 18th birthday started off right. Seeing his smile is all I wanted. Right before lunch I received a text from him that he had left me something in the mail room. It was a present. He remembered the little things I told him. My favorite snack was popcorn, I disliked the color pink (he bought a pink bag, but it was cute.) Also inside the bag was a card. A card that could make any girl fall to their knees. Now I won't spoil what he wrote, but I will tell you this, it was the best birthday card I had received in 18 years. So, I met him at the dock and in the most awkward, nerdy, nervous way possible he asked to move this into a "more serious relationship." We were officially dating. It felt weird, that's my boyfriend?

Our first date is one for the books, that's for sure. We spent almost two and a half hours at the doctor, so he could get a pill to lower the swelling from a bee sting. Do I regret it at all? Absolutely not. We spent almost two hours in the car on the way back to my house. We tried to go hiking, but it didn't work out. What did work out is all the giggles he gave me. We went out to eat and for the first time I truly looked into his eyes. I couldn't look away. I just want to dive in them, they are so warm and draw you in. Then he had to leave, and it was one of the hardest goodbyes I have done. He didn't come back to camp and was done for the summer. I still had two weeks left but all I could think about was him. The feeling he gave me, the way he made me smile. He took me on a date to Munsinger in Saint Cloud. This was the first time he held my hand. I remember the feeling as if it was yesterday. His warm hands interlocked mine and I felt safe. I felt at home. I didn't want the feeling to go away. Finally, it came to the point where he was going to meet my family. We went out to Applebee's with my dad and stepmom, I had the usual, chicken strips but so did Allen. Great minds think alike, huh? I was freaking out, but there was no reason to. My parents loved him. We were sitting in the car. His fingers were interlocked with mine. The rain was rolling down the windshield. The car was warm, the perfect setting to fall asleep in. I couldn't close my eyes though, I was drawn. Drawn to Allen. I looked at him and realized, I truly do love him.

Allen is my best friend. My partner in crime. The person I want to tell my greatest dreams to but also my fears in life. I look at him and I feel at home. I see a future in his eyes. With him by my side I feel like I can accomplish anything. He draws me closer to

Jesus. He shows me what real love is. He makes me want to reach my dreams. And although this distance between us is hard, not being with him would be harder. Not a day goes by that I don't thank God for giving me him. I am absolutely, undoubtedly, in love with him. To quote one of my favorite songs, Can't help falling in love by Elvis Presley, "wise men say, only fools rush in, but I can't help falling in love with you."

Chapter VI: Pretty Little Fools

Should I Date a Non-believer?

One of the hardest questions single believers will face is whether or not they should date a non-believer. It is not an easily answered question, and as with all relationships, the human aspects of the heart weigh heavily on the decision.

The Bible actually addresses this very subject, 2 Corinthians 6:14 says,

"Don't team up with those who are unbelievers. How can righteousness be a partner with wickedness? How can light live with darkness?"

Though dating is not marriage, it is the precursor of marriage and in mature relationships rests on the back of the mind. Any dating relationship neglecting to think about marriage really has very shallow intents, and in many ways, is a waste of time for both parties, but that is another discussion for another time. But the concept of "teaming up" is important to recognize. Your future spouse should be your best teammate, but if your teammate isn't even playing the same sport as you, chances are your team will fall apart.

Not all unbelievers are bad people whatsoever, nor are they beyond finding a relationship with God, but that is not your job in dating them. So many people have convinced themselves in "missionary dating" where they hope that in dating a non-believer they will have an influence on that person and they will come to faith. Though this has seen success in some cases, it is rarely the norm. Jesus did not call His followers to go and date the unsaved, but He did call them to befriend and minister to them. This can all be done outside of a romantic relationship and if anything, adding romance to the equation would only take away from the intent to bring the person into a relationship with Christ.

A simple answer of, "don't do it" does not take away the desire in the heart. Often times it can even be a tool of temptation against a believer to compromise their beliefs and go for what they can see and what is easily accessible. We live in an instant gratification seeking world, and to have a tangible and easy relationship at hand can often be extremely hard to give up.

In a moment of a personal story firsthand, I found myself in this exact spot with a man I honestly had come to love. We never had dated, rather, had been close friends for many years. Each time I thought something would begin, it seemed an obstacle arose, and I eventually gave up and moved on, for it was not a relationship where God had planted the seed to endure. I was about to move across the country to Minnesota when I was asked to dinner by this close friend. Being a very blonde girl at heart, I thought it was just dinner and not a date, but I was very wrong. He and I are both mature adults and both in a season of life where marriage is more of the intent of relationships than just summer crushes, and he implied his desire to marry. More closely, what a good wife and mother I would be. I was sitting there with literally everything a girl wants to hear of how lovely, smart, kind, and wonderful she is and all, but a ring offered with a horrendous catch in hand. I knew he didn't love God, and I knew God didn't want this for me.

The real root of it all is if someone does not love God first and most, they cannot love you properly. God is love, so if a person does not know the Highest form of love, they cannot know how to love truly and fully. CS Lewis said, "To love you as I should, I must worship God as Creator. When I have learnt to love God better than my earthly dearest, I shall love my earthly dearest better than I do now. In so far as I learn to love my earthly dearest at the expense of God and instead of God, I shall be moving towards the state in which I shall not love my earthly dearest at all. When first things are put first, second things are not suppressed but increased."

What Lewis was getting at was that in order to love to the highest expression of love and love correctly, we must love through Christ. If the person you are considering does not even believe in God, he does not know that love. You cannot share what you do not have, so lacking that most important aspect will only lead to heartache, disappointment, and downfall.

This is not to say that a Christian man will be perfect, he is still a human, but he will have that accountability backing him. He will know that as a husband he is called to love his wife as Christ loves the church (Ephesians 5) which means even to the point of death loving her.

How my story ended was I went back to my car and screamed at God. I sobbed all the way home and threw a little fit. Real mature, eh? But the fleshy parts of me had wanted to be with him so badly, it was a literal battle between my spirit and flesh. I prayed and as He is prone to doing, God answered in the Word. My Bible literally opened to 2 Corinthians 6 and I read the verse that contained my answer so clearly. It took time, prayer, and the Holy Spirit to help my flesh let go of what it wanted to cling to, for I did love him, just not through God. God is gracious, and I can firsthand attest that He will help when we ask.

In choosing to not "team up" with a non-believer, we sacrifice to God. What we sacrifice begins as the desires of the flesh and the instant gratification that comes from having something right away, but what we gain is worth far more. What we gain is protection from a sliding door path of eventual frustration, heartache, and feeling unfulfilled. What we gain is time back for not wasting time on our own follies. What we gain is looking to God to lead us in the right path for our lives. The man of your dreams may not come the day after you sacrifice the relationship with a non-believer, but God will. God will direct your path and make it straight, even when you don't understand (Proverbs 3:5-6). God will not leave you disappointed, "Then you will know that I am the Lord; those who hope in me will not be disappointed." (Isaiah 49:23), and He will bless you ahead.

What if you have already found yourself on the flip side of this instant relationship and very burned? There is hope for you too, just like there is hope for me. For God promises perhaps the greatest promise of the Bible, Romans 8:28, "And we know that in all things God works for the good of those who love him, who have been called according to his purpose."

Take it to God and wait for an answer. He will give you the best route, "I am the Lord your God, who teaches you what is best for you, who directs you in the way you should go." Isaiah 48:17.

He will not disappoint you, and He will bless you for trusting Him over your own flesh. It won't be easy, but in the end, it will be worth it.

Prayer:

Dear Lord,

Give us courage to believe You will not disappointed. Give us courage to hand over every relationship to You.

In Jesus name,
Amen

Romans 8:28-Fitz

It is honestly the story of grace that the story where you messed up becomes the foundational story of a later testimony. A story in which God took the muck you made, and shapes it into a beautiful vase. For me, it was a boy.

His name was Fitz. When it all began, we were barely acquaintances. He and I both attended a Young Adults group in college, and for a solid few months he was just that skinny dude who played drums. Time passed, and I ended up joining the Praise and Worship Team, and that is where we really began to bond. We both had a true love of music, and most of our favorite bands were the same as well. It's a typical girl meets boy story for the most part, but in truth it was so much more complicated that just that sort of label. In fact, labels were what got us in trouble most, there wasn't one.

See, we were never really, "official" but the truth was we were far more serious than most

Facebook status couples. Truthfully, we were more serious than most couples who end up married. But that is the thing with an addition, you don't realize you're addicted until you're in too deep and things get real, but it's time I continue with the story.

Months passed, and Fitz and I became closer and closer. He was a drummer and we played gigs together and of course Worship Team. We saw each other nearly every day, but if we didn't we communicated constantly, excessively. Mornings were always greeted with a, "good morning" text and nights usually ended around 2 AM falling asleep with the phone in my hand. I honestly do not know how I graduated with honors with the time I devoted to Fitz. But addictions are powerful.

Part of me chooses to play the innocent victim card that I was a tragically lonely girl starved for attention and desiring friends, and though that is true, it didn't make it right all I fed into it all. Nor did it help that the one pursuing me was obsessive and a tad manipulative too. But I let it persist.

The guilt weighed heavily upon me. Sleepless nights of tossing and turning and begging God for an answer, though the answer was as clear as the blue in Fitz's eyes. Yet I continued to choose momentary satisfaction. Isn't that the real root of sin? Selfishness. The selfish desire to continue on with something you know is wrong, yet it satisfies a hole in your heart, so you persist.

It is interesting how memories work. The polaroids in my head depict so many different occasions with the same feeling: slight satisfaction smothered in regret. Like the night we went to the Jazz Ball. I spent hours the evening before working to get my eye makeup just right for him. The next evening provided an existential meltdown at the hand of fake eyelashes. Then came the ball. I felt a princess the way he adoringly stared, we trembled as our hands we held to dance. I taught him how to swing dance that night, and he taught me how to let go.

Another polaroid is us on a beach for three hours knee deep in thought and waist deep in quick sand. Yet another the Christmas gift he gave me, and the moment where I knew I loved him. The ironic thing about relationships is that they are marked by snapshot memories, both good and bad. Looking back, it's like I could shake a snow globe holding us both in that moment. It was a few days before Christmas and we were in the middle of a McDonald's. He nervously placed his hand on the back of his neck rubbing it like he would with a slight blush hue upon his cheeks. It was a small book of poems by Robert Frost, mentioning that he remembered me saying in passing how he was my favorite author. Additionally, there was a mixed CD of songs for me to listen to on my Christmas travels up North with a track-by-track explanation for each song and the emotions he hoped I would feel for each song. Thoughtfulness is my love language, and he knocked it out of the park on this one. I caught my own tongue looking in his eyes that night that I loved him, for in fact I did. Oddly that snapshot memory is like a snow globe, something I'd place on a shelf and enjoy looking at every once in a while, but at peace that it is not my current reality. For every relationship has snapshots such as these, but it also holds snapshots of memories and stains one would like to erase, but needed to develop character and clarity.

As such, there was always the pressure for, "more." I recall the day I *met the parents* when there were the twenty questions rounds, curiosity of his sisters, and a moment from his parents. Another time a dinner invitation by his aunt included an inquisitive request to know what kind of engagement ring I would desire. There is a line between pursing and pressure, and Fitz had passed that line miles before. Yet I was young and naive...and he was persistent.

God did try and separate us. Whether it was the constant spats we would have or the fact that he finished school and could not find a job, not even an entry level job, that caused him to move over two hours away. It was the last day where things broke down...for the first time....

He was to move the next day, so we planned a day doing everything we loved to do. We went to

Lamplighter's Coffee in Cary Town, a photography stop in Midlothian mines, his first experience with sushi, and topped it off watching, *Frozen* where even in the movie God was trying to tell me not to fall for Hans. Then came time to say goodbye. He held me in his arms for half an hour. Tears cascaded down his face as he expressed his true feelings. I had known for some time he loved me, and I knew the night he gave me that book of poems that I loved him, but it was the first time in which we didn't walk around what we had been holding back for nearly a year. The silence said far more than words in the hollow chill of that January evening. Then I left.

I knew it was wrong, I knew God didn't want me with him. I knew everything I had fallen into was worldly and not pursuing God. Just because we were both Christians never meant we were truly pursing Him together. I tried to put a stop to it after that night, used the excuse of the distance, but we both knew we were not friends any longer. I remember sobbing and fighting on the phone with him at Einstein Brother's Bagels that next morning. Yet he continued to persist, and I let him.

We exchanged handwritten letters multiple times a week in the mail. They contained pleadings to become more serious, reminders of the closeness we shared. I kept them for years in a box, there must have been over thirty letters from him all saturated with reminders of our relationship, of his life or mine, of inside jokes, of the life we shared.

Anyway, things became even more serious after that. I visited the beach, and he visited me in Richmond. Each time was marked with a more serious move and so many near misses of a physical aspect of the relationship beyond holding hands or playing footsies. It was shortly after me crying in his car after Captain America that I was given an ultimatum.

I planned to say yes. In fact, I wrote an entire letter sharing that I had not gotten a clear *no* (well, it wasn't written in the sky) and so why the heck not? But the morning came for me to tell him, and God hit me over the head so hard I had never had such a headache. It was clearly spoken on my heart that I would, "not receive the man promised if I said yes to Fitz." With that, I said, "no." I saw true colors, I learned and saw the complete truth of who I was to him. I felt abandoned, beguiled, alone, and like a B word for breaking his heart. I told him the truth, that God had given me a dream many years prior of the man whom I was to marry, and it wasn't Fitz. Sadly, that was not believed although it was completely true. That conversation still to this day echoes like ghosts in the catacombs of my memory. He implied not to contact him unless I was dying (which at that time with my health was an actual possibility) and we said goodbye. Alone.

I will admit I was angry with God for the months to come. I spent a mission trip trying to find out the truth about that dream three years earlier. I went off the deep end and began hanging out with less than noble people and making poor decisions. I learned the sole message in an alcohol bottle is emptiness. I truly became Jonah after completing his mission-angry and bitter at God. But it was there that He came to reach me.

It was December 22nd and I woke up in tears. I wanted to kill myself. I didn't want to be on this earth anymore, but it was in that bottom pit that I saw the Light when I looked up. In a tearful surrender, I fell to my knees asking Him to come save me. I told Him that every single time I tried to *figure it out myself* or *do it my way,* I ended up alone and in regret, so I asked Him to take back the pilot's seat, and He did. Instantly the Holy Spirit overcame me like the gentle fall of rain. I was blanketed in peace and love, and I felt no shame anymore. No regret, we were on the right path.

The weeks that followed also were full of revelations and pure grace. It took surrendering Fitz to gain the truth. It took me handing Him a stone to receive a pearl of hope. The months and years that passed that fateful day have been one hell of an adventure. He pruned me and sanctified me. As John 15 says, ""I am the true vine, and my Father is the gardener. He cuts off every branch in me that bears no fruit, while every branch that does bear fruit he prunes[a] so that it will be even more fruitful. You are already clean because of the word I have spoken to you. Remain in me, as I also remain in you. No branch can bear fruit by itself; it must remain in the vine. Neither can you bear fruit unless you remain in me." He pruned even the good aspects of me in order for me to become more fruitful later on. At the time, I yelled and screamed and protested for it hurts when you are torn apart. But as Hosea 6:1 says,

> ""Come, let us return to the Lord.
> He has torn us to pieces
> but he will heal us;
> he has injured us
> but he will bind up our wounds."

He tore me apart in order to restore me to greater glory for His purpose, and for that I am truly and eternally grateful.

That is the Romans 8:28 of this story. I deserved to be shamed by God for my direct disobedience. I deserved to be cast out and not receive the promise, but He remained faithful. The time that followed was no easy journey, but it produced the primary character of the woman I have become. Romans 5 shares, "And we boast in the hope of the glory of God. Not only so, but we also glory in our sufferings, because we know that suffering produces perseverance; perseverance, character; and character, hope. And hope does not put us to shame, because God's love has been poured out into our hearts through the Holy Spirit, who has been given to us."

My point is this: it is worth it, because of Him. Not because of the promise of a husband, or even the person you will become, but it is worth it because of Jesus Christ Himself. For He is far greater than anything that we use to coax and Band-Aid the holes in our hearts with. We use a temporary Band-Aid, but was occurs is bacteria that makes the infection far worse. It is through His healing blood that we are truly made whole and white again. I cannot promise it will be easy, but it will be worth it. Romans 8:28 makes that clear, that, "And we know that in all things God works for the good of those who love him, who have been called according to his purpose."

Dating Blooper Reel

It is a huge rarity to find someone who does not have a few funny or horrible dating stories up their sleeves, but they are always hilarious nevertheless. This chapter isn't really anything to help you along, but perhaps just a reminder that if you have gone on a bad date, you are not alone.

My personal one to share is a date with a guy named Blake. I met Blake at my good friend's wedding a few years back. It began at the rehearsal dinner, I was attempting to stay awake after a long day of wedding venue set-up when in walks in Captain America's doppelgänger. He was tall, handsome, and had a smile that could melt a popsicle in a blizzard. He wasn't in the wedding, so he didn't sit with the wedding party and directly after we were rushed over to the hotel. I still got my chance, it was just after the wedding.

The wedding was on the beautiful Virginia countryside and being the amateur photographer I am, I took the great opportunity to snatch some pictures after pictures were finished. As I was walking back, sure enough he was standing there playing corn hole with his friend. For those of you who do not know what corn hole is, it's a game where you toss bean bags into a wooden palette to score points. I suck at it usually. He smiled back at me and invited me to play, me blushingly admitting to my poor coordination with such sports. In the most suave moment of my entire life, I threw the bag and it hit the target the first time, along with Blake's interest. Being coy, I shrugged it off as beginner's luck. We were interrupted by the cutting of the cake when he began inquiring about me, how I knew Bailey and Bryan, among other things. It was soon to leave, and he asked how to contact me. Now I never give my number out to boys, just a solid rule I have. So, I told him to find me on Facebook, quite a challenge for someone with a name like Cally.

Sure enough, within two hours a friend request sat in my inbox and we were set to go out on our first date the next week. I drove back up from college (it was my senior year) and we met at the movies. This is where his first foul ball came into play, he made me pay my own way....and he wouldn't let me choose the movie. Regardless, it was a decent time. I honestly do not even recall the movie, that's how unremarkable that was. Afterwards we walked to TGIFriday's where he insisted we sit indoors....at the bar....and I froze. At least he bought my iced tea. It was a date with good enough conversation and all, so I agreed to a second date and gave a good old-fashioned side hug goodbye.

He would text me constantly and was very forward, but I brushed it off that I was being apprehensive too much because I had been alone too much, and it was sweet. He promised to take me to one of the nicest French restaurants in town, something I certainly did not expect (I freaking love Applebee's honestly) but of course I said that would be lovely. I wore the cutest little sundress I had and spruced up my long brown hair and met him downtown. He proceeded to share that he wasn't that hungry after all, and after walking around aimlessly for half hour, suggested just ice cream. Which was fine, but I hadn't eaten since lunch, so I was pretty hungry. The conversation on that date was a lot less pleasurable. He dropped how he had his grandmother's jewelry and if, "I was good" maybe I would get some of that. The conversation was pretty one sided, and to top it off when I asked what his plans later were he proceeded to tell me he was going to Hooters, "Because I like their wings, *wink*" Immediately I asked if he was serious, and he was! I left. Got home and he had some bogus Facebook post about what a great date he had been on and now he was enjoying wings, and I resolved to stop dating body builders. The moral of my story is, don't settle for slimy jerks.

Don't Settle for the Bowl of Soup

We live in an age of instant gratification. I'm guilty of wanting what I want when I want it too, which is why I settled for the iPhone 8 Plus over the X, so I could get it a month early, and then now am trying to sell it because it wasn't worth it. I settled for what I could grab easily, rather than the prize. But life isn't about phones.

This is nothing new of wanting instant gratification. In fact, there is someone in the Bible who gave up his happiness in life for what was easily attainable.

In Genesis 25 we hear the story of Jacob and Esau,

"Once when Jacob was cooking some stew, Esau came in from the open country, famished. He said to Jacob, "Quick, let me have some of that red stew! I'm famished!" Jacob replied, "First sell me your birthright."
"Look, I am about to die," Esau said. "What good is the birthright to me?"
But Jacob said, "Swear to me first." He swore an oath to him, selling his birthright to Jacob. Then Jacob gave Esau some bread and some lentil stew. He ate and drank, and then got up and left. Esau despised his birthright."

Esau saw what was quick and easily satisfying, but gave up his birthright. In this family, birthrights were a big deal, and he didn't value it at all. In the same way, don't we squander important aspects of our own lives? Go for what is easily attainable and will satisfy for a time, all to find that down the road it will in vain?

To stick along with the topic of this chapter, let's talk about relationships. When everyone seems to be pairing up and you can't go on Facebook without seeing another engagement or baby announcement, it can be so tempting to grab at what is easily attained. It can be so easy to sell our birthrights and lose out on future joy.

Think about it this way, does soup taste better from being cooked in a microwave or a slow cooker? Be honest.

Relationships are like slow cookers, the longer you wait for the ultimate, the better it will be and gosh worth the wait. Don't sell out for the microwave marriage that is built up of sloppy leftovers and leaves you with an aftertaste of "good enough."

God has different paths and stories for us all. He has seasons for doors to open, and if your season is early on, there is nothing wrong with that whatsoever. What I am getting at here is do not settle. It's never worth it. Esau settled for a bowl of stew over an honored life.

More than likely you know if you are settling, even if you won't admit it out loud. There's that gut feeling deep down that you're selling out for that stew, when holding out a little longer would be so much more worth it. So why do we stay then? Is it the imminent fear of being alone? Is it the lack of trusting that God actually does have someone for us? Is it that we don't trust God deep down?

What if it's all of the above?

A good friend of mine once said that when God plants these seeds of desires within our hearts, it is good, for He is good. But in our human nature, we grow impatient that it's not in our timing, it's in His timing. So, we get frustrated and angry at Him. We feel disappointed and like He has let us down. This is natural and its pure humanness to rebel against God and wrestle with Him, but it's in the listening and letting Him work that the real growth comes. See, it's a process, and if we just surrender and allow Him to work in us, we realize He is not cruel for making us wait. He is not slow to fulfill as we humans would count slowness, rather He is working by transforming us from our inner being for our highest good, and His highest glory. Don't resist the transformation. Don't settle for the stew.

For a personal response in that, I was on the path to settling. I think you look around you and see all your friends getting married and in this sort of dreamland, and then you start to doubt that you're worthy of that happiness. So, you settle. You begin in your heart to settle for you know is not God's best, or your best. You convince yourself that you are actually too picky and that your aspirations are far too high, and you convince yourself that you're worth so little. Don't do this. Don't settle for good enough.

Prayer:

Dear Lord,

Please work in us. Please help us be patient and never settle for a bowl of soup, but instead for what You have for us. Help us surrender to Your timing and Your call. We know You always reward obedience, in Your time, not ours.

In Jesus name,

Amen

Chapter VII: Active Waiting

Active Waiting

Active waiting sounds a bit like an oxymoron. The act of being patient and waiting, yet being active may sound foreign to some. In Cycle Bar (think Soul Cycle) there is a term called, "active recovery" which is where one recovers from a massive climb without stopping. In the same way, it is possible to actively wait. It is possible to intentionally, actively wait.

Being intentional is a way of life. It puts the One you serve first, and it makes an effort to in every way mold your life to focus on Christ, with every action. James 5:12 calls to, "let your "yes" be yes and your "no" be no" This means intentionally living in such a way that you make the *choice* to let the major and minor decisions of your life reflect and honor God in every way. Living with intention will always yield abundant fruit, for even if we make mistakes God is working with that spirit, that heart, and those intentions to bless the Kingdom, and in turn He will bless you. James 5:16 shares, "The prayer of a righteous person is powerful and effective." God is able to look past our masks, look past the walls we put up, and look into the deep intentions of our spirits. When we live in such an intentional way as to bless Him, He supplies where we lack, He guides, He blesses. Even in the waiting periods of life.

If God has called you into a season of waiting, it is never to just sit like Rapunzel in a tower waiting for an answer or a Prince. In fact, it is in those waiting seasons that the most work can take place. The greatest activity can occur. The root defining growth can occur.

The root determines the fruit. The deeper the root, the more abundant the fruit will be. Jesus speaks of it in the Parable of the Scattering Seeds in Matthew 13, "Listen! A farmer went out to plant some seeds. As he scattered them across his field, some seeds fell on a footpath, and the birds came and ate them. Other seeds fell on shallow soil with underlying rock. The seeds sprouted quickly because the soil was shallow. But the plants soon wilted under the hot sun, and since they didn't have deep roots, they died. Other seeds fell among thorns that grew up and choked out the tender plants. Still other seeds fell on fertile soil, and they produced a crop that was thirty, sixty, and even a hundred times as much as had been planted! Anyone with ears to hear should listen and understand."

The seeds with the deep roots produced an exponential crop. This is what waiting and enduring will also do when intentionally done right. When you intentionally seek to wait actively, the roots will deepen and the fruit will be far more abundant. It is ironic how gardening will indeed prove the verses read even a hundred times. This weekend the weather finally permitted for me to get around to gardening some. While planting the seed I was reminded of a story a dear friend shared with me recently. She told how last year she planted some seeds, making sure they weren't too close to the surface and had plenty of opportunity for sun and water. Week after week, nothing sprouted up. She kept tending to it every day with sun and water, but it seemed to no avail. One day she had the thought to brush some of the dirt when she saw that the plant had actually been growing the entire time. Not only had it been growing, but its roots went very, very deep. The plant didn't show on the surface, but the roots were ensuring that it would last for years to come. It had such deep roots that even the strongest of storms would not overtake the plant. It's the same way with our lives, we may pray about something for even years on end and feel we have nothing on the outside to show for it, but take into consideration that God is planting some seed and growing roots. He is growing the roots in the situation, and He is growing your roots in Him. Don't give up just because you can't see it yet, the deeper the root, the stronger the tree. This is active waiting.

Think of it like a hallway. If you are in that hallway between seasons, you can actively wait and create something beautiful. Paint the hallways, use the time to express yourself as creatively as possible. Take hold of the blank canvas of time and create something unique in every way. That is how this book was made. I've been in an active waiting season for some time now, but what is humbling is that God has taken this time to not only grow my roots richly in Him, but to create this book. Time to create meaningful and intentional relationships with my little flock of birds I mentor as well. This book was inspired by their challenges and questions, as well as a few of my own. If it were not for this waiting period God has given me, this would have never been written.

Active waiting is a time in which the work behind the scenes, the work deep within can flourish. Don't just endure such a season, richly bloom within its borders.

Prayer:

Dear Lord,

Thank You for knowing better than us. Thank You that even in those seasons where we resist with all of our flesh, You know better. You know that such seasons can be used to actively grow, actively learn, and actively flourish within You. Help us live with intention, help us when we lack, and let each and every season in our lives be used for Your glory and our benefit-to know You all the more.

In Christ's name,

Amen.

Dear Future Husband

Perhaps what you are specifically *waiting* for is more of a who.... a future husband who. The blessing is you can actively wait for your husband as well. This doesn't merely mean avoiding dating those fleshy relationships that you know for certain are not of God (which are important), but also communicating your heart to your husband perhaps before you even meet him.

For nearly a decade I've written letters to my future husband. They began in a journal, then two journals, then slews of letters. Running total right now is around 250.... I've been actively waiting for a while. What is beautiful is what those letters hold. They have the ability to convey heart, intent, and growth throughout the years. From milestones, he wasn't there for to ideas for apple trees at our home to sincere written prayers for him-they're all there. Imagine how beautiful it will be the day your husband reads them. The day he sees how intentional you were to pray for him, to think of him, to love him before you two even met. It is like a time capsule you can hand your husband one day.

These letters are all your own. They can be in prayer form, diary form, or anything you really want. You can wait to fill his name in later for the, "Dear _____" part, or simply put, "Dear Future Husband." Make the letters your own. They are a lovely representation of conveying your heart to his heart, one letter at a time.

Especially do not forget to write such letters leading up to your wedding as well. Save these letters forever, and one day when you are both graying and life is hard, you can both recall that fresh, bright-eyed love that was bottled up for a time, like a fine wine. Savored, saved, and significant solely for him.

Prayer:

Dear Lord,

Thank You for the future spouse of the young woman reading this book. We pray for him even now. We pray that the heart of the woman reading this will patiently wait for him, pray for him, and truly know that he is worth waiting for. We pray for his heart for You, we pray that daily he picks up his cross and follows You. We pray he is growing and becoming the mighty man of Christ You intended him to be. We pray for the letters that will be written for his heart from his loving wife.

In Jesus name,
Amen

Off the Cuff

If you're ever feeling down on your life, remember some kid was benched so a dog could take his place in, *Air Bud.*

Ruth Before Boaz

This final section of this chapter is for the girls who have not yet found or met their spouses. This is a chapter for the girls still waiting for their Boaz to wake up and realize they're the one. This one is for the girls who are waiting in that hallway for God to open the door into the next chapter of their lives. This chapter is for the girls with a heart like Ruth.

Ruth wasn't just your typical woman. She faced adversity, loss, grief, and heartache, but remained steadfast and faithful through it all. She knew that her God would be faithful by her....and He was.

Ruth's story begins with a life chapter ending. Her husband of ten years suddenly dies along with her brother-in-law and father-in-law. Ruth, Naomi (her mother-in-law), and Orpah (sister-in-law who I obviously picture in my head as Oprah) are all left widows. The secure and safe life they had come to know was shattered. They must have felt so lonely, forgotten, and unsure of where to go next. Naomi even said her new nickname should be, "Mara" which means, "bitter." Orpah decides to go back to her father's family for refuge, and Naomi suggests Ruth do the same. This moment right here is the definitive moment that will cause a domino effect for the rest of Ruth's life. You see, she did not see her role in Naomi's family to be temporary. It was not some entry-level job she was using as a stepping stone. It was not just a chapter or season in her life, Naomi was family. She was committed to God to serve in that family until death. Let's look to the text:

"Look," said Naomi, "your sister-in-law is going back to her people and her gods. Go back with her.

But Ruth replied, "Don't urge me to leave you or to turn back from you. Where you go I will go, and where you stay I will stay. Your people will be my people and your God my God. Where you die I will die, and there I will be buried. May the Lord deal with me, be it ever so severely, if even death separates you and me." When Naomi realized that Ruth was determined to go with her, she stopped urging her."

This is mark one of where we can take note
from Ruth. She was loyal to the position God had
called her to. God had chosen her to marry into
Naomi's family, and Ruth saw that as a commitment
until her death. She chose to faithfully live out the
position God had called her to for that time in her
life-even if it was not the preferred or the encouraged
by others. Let's make this personal. Has there ever
been a time in your own life that you knew with no
shadow of doubt God was calling you to stay or go
into a position, and you received little to no support?
Everyone called you crazy for staying or going,
everyone looked down on you for that? Perhaps it
would mean a less comfortable life, perhaps it would
ensue hardships and storms. Perhaps it would be the
more radical choice-but it was the God given
obedience choice. This is where Ruth was. Sure, Ruth
could have gone home like Orpah and lived a safe
little quiet life back home with her parents. She
would have received little to no harassment from her
family or peers. It would have been a safe little life-
but because she was obedient to God's call even when

it made no sense to those around her, she was blessed. You see, Ruth was no ordinary woman. Ruth, we will see had a very important destiny that hinged completely on her obedience in season. Let's keep going.

She continues to live out life with Naomi, working hard for the necessities of life where she could. During this day in age rich land owners would allow for those less fortunate to eat off the corners of their land. Now it just so happened that one of those days Ruth was gathering food from the land of a man named Boaz. For cinematic quality, we can imagine Boaz as a silver fox. Not the youngest man, but certainly still a man that could make your heart flutter when he beams a million-dollar smile. In my head, he has the enduring swagger and looks of Eric Metaxas.... but I digress.

Anyway, Ruth sees Boaz for the first time. She is merely living out her daily duties of collecting food, when for a moment all of time stops in those eyes. Boaz takes notice of her as well, and inquires of her story. This is where we see their first interaction take place,

"So, Boaz said to Ruth, "My daughter, listen to me. Don't go and glean in another field and don't go away from here. Stay here with the women who work for me.[9] Watch the field where the men are harvesting, and follow along after the women. I have told the men not to lay a hand on you. And whenever you are thirsty, go and get a drink from the water jars the men have filled."

At this, she bowed down with her face to the ground. She asked him, "Why have I found such favor in your eyes that you notice me—a foreigner?"

Boaz replied, "I've been told all about what you have done for your mother-in-law since the death of your husband—how you left your father and mother and your homeland and came to live with a people you did not know before. May the Lord repay you for what you have done. May you be richly rewarded by the Lord, the God of Israel, under whose wings you have come to take refuge."

At first glance this is a bit of an odd first conversation, but when we really dig into it we see the respect Boaz gave her at first sight. He was moved by her integrity to fulfill her commitment to Naomi's family until *her* death, not only the death of her first husband. Boaz saw too the light of the Lord shining from her. By far my favorite line of Boaz is when he speaks of God taking Ruth, "under Whose wings you have come to take refuge." Gah! This is stunning. Boaz was taken aback by Ruth not merely for her looks, but because she made the *choice* to take refuge under God's wings. She chose to live her life in such an intentional way that she was committed to God-not the consensus of her peers-for refuge, strength, and direction. In the most respectful way Boaz can convey this, he allows Ruth to gather from his own personal fields. He gives her permission to drink from his own personal water supply (which we know was Dasani Water). Boaz even then wanted to take care of her, not dictate what she would do, but offer up everything he could in the most respectful way.

Ruth then travels home to Naomi to tell of her day, and Naomi is all too ready to stir the pot. This next part is going to sound a little strange, but just keep with the story. It will all make sense once we flesh it out.

"One day Ruth's mother-in-law Naomi said to her, "My daughter, I must find a home for you, where you will be well provided for. Now Boaz, with whose women you have worked, is a relative of ours. Tonight, he will be winnowing barley on the threshing floor. Wash, put on perfume, and get dressed in your best clothes. Then go down to the threshing floor, but don't let him know you are there until he has finished eating and drinking. When he lies down, note the place where he is lying. Then go and uncover his feet and lie down. He will tell you what to do." (Ruth 3:1-4)

Naomi told Ruth to pursue Boaz. She noted to dress in her very best, and to sincerely and honestly go to him with her intentions. Though it is not explicitly said, I think it is safe to assume Ruth was quite taken with Boaz, and it was Naomi's hope to encourage this relationship to happen. Now at first glance when we read verse 4, we cannot help but think it sounds a little strange. Kind of a, "hey, I just met you, and this is crazy...but I'll lie in your bed, marry me maybe?" It's not as promiscuous as it sounds. Ruth was actually humbling herself to Boaz's feet to show him reverence and show him respect. This was a risky move in itself being an unmarried woman pursuing out a man of such importance, but this is evidence of God having a hand on every single detail. God led Naomi's heart to encourage Ruth to put herself out there for Boaz, to confront him and share her own feelings, and God filled in the rest. Obedience to God may not always make sense and often can be incredible daring and risky, but if it is from the call of the Lord Himself it will in the end turn out well. John 13:7 rings true in this instance, "you may not understand what I am doing now, but one day you will."

Thankfully we are not left on a cliff hanger. What happens next is a God weaved story of grace and blessings.

""Who are you?" he asked.

"I am your servant Ruth," she said. "Spread the corner of your garment over me, since you are a guardian-redeemer[b] of our family."

"The Lord bless you, my daughter," he replied. "This kindness is greater than that which you showed earlier: You have not run after the younger men, whether rich or poor. And now, my daughter, don't be afraid. I will do for you all you ask. All the people of my town know that you are a woman of noble character. Although it is true that I am a guardian-redeemer of our family, there is another who is more closely related than I. Stay here for the night, and in the morning if he wants to do his duty as your guardian-redeemer, good; let him redeem you. But if he is not willing, as surely as the Lord lives I will do it. Lie here until morning."

So she lay at his feet until morning, but got up before anyone could be recognized; and he said, "No one must know that a woman came to the threshing floor."

He also said, "Bring me the shawl you are wearing and hold it out." When she did so, he poured into it six measures of barley and placed the bundle on her. Then he[c] went back to town."

There is an abundance of symbolism here. A guardian-redeemer was someone in charge of caring for the family. This meant redeeming the family in crisis, much like how God does for us. We are His children, and when we are in a crisis He is there to comfort and help us. Ruth had another guardian-redeemer by law, so that is why it was even more noble of Boaz to step up and courageously ask for Ruth's hand in marriage.

Boaz shows his upstanding morals again here. He had the opportunity to take advantage of Ruth and sleep with her-but instead he respects her. He does not defile her reputation. He shows that respect to her by keeping her honor held safe and secure. Also, can we note how he fed her breakfast with all the barely he sent her off with. Bonus points.

Back at the ranch Naomi is all ready to hear how things went. Ruth explains how Boaz must ask permission in order to marry her, again he showed her respect and respected her family by ensuring what he intended to do was proper. Naomi shares in 3:18, "Then Naomi said, "Wait, my daughter, until you find out what happens. For the man will not rest until the matter is settled today." This is a reminder that at times obedience will be left at a cliff hanger. You will have done all that you can do, but it rests in the Lord's hands how the outcome will come and how He will move and work in the hearts of men to fulfill His purposes.

Ruth's obedience paid off. Boaz is given approval to marry Ruth, and truly what happens next is lovelier than even the most tear jerking *Hallmark* movie or greatest of fairytales.

" So Boaz took Ruth and she became his wife. When he made love to her, the Lord enabled her to conceive, and she gave birth to a son. The women said to Naomi: "Praise be to the Lord, who this day has not left you without a guardian-redeemer. May he become famous throughout Israel! He will renew your life and sustain you in your old age. For your daughter-in-law, who loves you and who is better to you than seven sons, has given him birth."

Boaz marries Ruth. God blesses she who was without child, with a beautiful son. A son of promise, a son who is indeed the fruit of obedience. Obedience always ushers forth a harvest, but in God's timing, not ours. We see those who encountered this miracle have changed hearts as well. Those who stood in skepticism of Ruth and Naomi at the beginning of our story are now humbled by the work of the Lord, even saying how His name would be made famous by the miracles taken place in Ruth and Naomi's lives.

Ruth's story does not merely end here, in fact her obedience would create a domino effect that would bless the entire universe until the end of age. You see, Ruth gave birth to a baby named Obed. Obed had a son named Jesse, who had a son named David. David would be made King of all of Israel, and have a heart truly after God. David would even come to see what his own great-grandfather saw in verse 2:12 of, "May you be richly rewarded by the Lord, the God of Israel, under whose wings you have come to take refuge" for in Psalm 91:4 he shares, "He will cover you with his feathers, and under His wings you will find refuge; His faithfulness will be your shield and rampart." The actions and heart of his ancestors had a domino effect on his own understanding and worldview. This goes to show that the obedience of even one person-even one woman-can affect the course of history for the Kingdom for all of time. You see, David would be in the lineage of Jesus. God knew Ruth would obedient to the call upon her life, and He chose her for such a mission, such a life.

Do not regard your beginnings as your ending. Your story is not even finished when you leave this earth, for the impact you have on others goes on and on forever, just like love. A quote I came across years ago has always stuck with me, "in life be a snowflake: leave a mark, but no stain." The way you live your life, your obedience, even in small things leaves marks. These marks effect those in your surroundings, and that legacy goes on and on. Do not believe your beginnings are in vain. Do not believe your obedience is in vain. God always blesses obedience, God always blesses good intentions, God always fulfills His purpose. It is up to us to be obedient like Ruth and trust even when the entire world is against us.

Prayer:

Dear Lord,

Thank You for noble women like Ruth. Thank you that we can truly look to them as role models in pursuit of Your calling. We pray that we will have the courage and bold temperaments to live fearlessly in service of Your call like Ruth. We pray for men after Your own heart like Boaz. We pray for Your glory throughout our lives.

In Jesus name,
Amen

Chapter VIII: Back to God

The Honor of Intercession

To preface how this chapter came to be, I must share a personal story of how this came to be. Praying for my future spouse has indeed become a constant. I pray for him not just daily, but throughout the day. After many years of praying, my resolve has grown weak here lately and I've become exhausted quite honestly. Nevertheless, the other day I was prayer journaling about him and right after I felt a very heavy and overwhelming weight upon my shoulders concerning my future husband. It drenched my mood like a wet coat, so heavy I could barely articulate words to say, let alone pray. Beset with this overcoming emotion, I was unable to shake it off as nothing. I began to pray for him, unsure what to pray. Thankfully we have a powerful intercessor Who is able to translate even moans into prayers to our Heavenly Father. I was given affirmation that my prayers were not in vain. In an act of selfish fleshy action, I quickly became bitter and complained. I retreated into my flesh to wish the man harm, but later was convicted of the error of my snap emotions thanks to my dear best friend, Charlotte.

The following day I came to the realization that it was not a burden, but an honored blessing for me to pray for this man. I was gifted a spiritual connection with this man to know to pray for him without an inkling of a sign beforehand that he needed intercession. This is the vital piece to remember when you are feeling depleted and exhausted for praying for someone: it is truly an honor.

There are 7 billion people on this planet, we will say 3.5 billion of them are women, so out of all those women, God chose me to pray for this man. Moreover, I was created for this. See, when God made the first woman, Eve, He had the first man, Adam in mind. The Bible says, "But for Adam no suitable helper was found. So, the Lord God caused the man to fall into a deep sleep; and while he was sleeping, he took one of the man's ribs and then closed up the place with flesh." (Genesis 2:19). God had Adam in mind while creating Eve, He knew Adam's heart for

He was the One Who made it, and made Eve perfectly suited for Adam. The same is true of your heart, dear reader. He had a specific man in mind when He made you, and likewise you were on His mind when creating this man. What a sincere honor it is truly to pray for this man meant for you. For God had you in mind in the creation of this man, and it is your honor and duty to pray for this man in your life. Paul says in 1 Corinthians 7:34-35, "But a married woman is concerned about the affairs of this world, that is, about how she can please her husband. I'm saying this for your benefit, not to put a noose around your necks, but to promote good order and unhindered devotion to the Lord." What this is meaning that a woman who is given or has a husband (this includes those praying for their man) are concerned with her husband. This is not a noose, but this is actually devotion to the Lord. The object of a godly marriage is through loving your spouse, you in turn fall more deeply in love with God. So, praying for your spouse in turn blesses God. It's honestly an honor if God gives you specifically someone to pray for.

For me, prayer is constant anyway, but this was not always the case. After God rejuvenated my relationship with Him, the wanderings of my mind were taken captive, and I began to navigate such thoughts in prayer and discussion to God. I also had very intentional intercession time for my future husband specifically as well. I had read many times how 40 days seemed to be a very holy number, such as Noah's flood or Jesus being led into the desert for 40 days to fast and pray. I prayed about how to conduct this prayer time, and learned through a Sermon and Scripture (Mark 6:48) that after Jesus fed the 5,000 he went off to pray in the hills. He instructed the Disciples to go on ahead of him, and around 3 AM he came to them, walking 3 or 4 miles into the water. It was here that the miracle of walking on the water, and calling Peter out to walk on the water as well occurred. Now the story of Jesus calling Peter out of the boat has always been near and dear to my heart, so I knew this was a wink for me. So, I set my alarm for 3 AM every morning and I prayed for 40 days. I prayed whatever the Spirit would lead for that day. At times it was for purity, other times for his parents (his mom specifically often times) or perhaps that he too would be awoken at 3 AM with the call to just be near God. I wrote down every night what I interceded for Him, along with the verses God provided in the wee hours of the morning. The last day was actually the day of a Solar Eclipse, a day in which the entire world stopped for a few brief moments to see the skies proclaim God's glory, and I do not think that a coincidence.

When I finished the 40 days, I did not stop praying. To be completely honest, I've been praying for him with every free thought for the past few years now. I am not saying that to sound righteous, or by any means like I am some saint, but in honesty it's for God more than it is for my future husband. You see, we have the beautiful opportunity to pray for others so that they bless the Kingdom. Eric Metaxas once conveyed in a keynote I attended how the real work we do is on this side of the Veil, once we are in Heaven, it is all praising and no sadness. All joy. So, it is vital that on this side of Heaven we strive to do as much as we can for the Kingdom. God blessed each of us with the incredible honor of being someone with a voice in the world and to those around us. I see that calling as a massive honor, but with a great weight along with it. I know my future spouse needs someone praying for him and supporting him, even from the sidelines. I cannot even imagine what all he will do in his life, but I pray over it. Your spouse is the exact same, they have a call and a place in ministry in their life. Even if they are working for a gas station, they have the beautiful call to scatter seeds for Christ. They need prayer, they need intercession, and if you are the (future) wife of this person, they need you. This is the job of a rib: to support the man to be upright towards God. So, with that, let us pray,

Dear Lord,

We praise Your Holy name. We know that You and You alone can work and guide and instruct hearts. We pray for our future spouses that You would guide them and work within them. We pray that in the same way, though intercession for others, You would work within us as well. We give our hearts to You for the changing and molding. We give to You the hearts of our spouses for changing and molding.

We give our breath, our day, and our role on this side of the Veil for Your glory.

In Jesus name,
Amen

Banks of Red Sea

Where are you today? Are you holding up during one of the worst seasons of your life? Are hopes and dreams and desires finding themselves to look completely impossible? Is everything you thought God would give you by now or you thought He promised looking to be the last possible thing that could happen right now? If so, you are at the banks of the Red Sea.

Nearly everyone knows the story of how God parted the Red Sea for the Israelites, but few know all the massive details that went into this miracle. See, after a long season of negotiations the Pharaoh of Egypt finally allowed the Israelites to go free. Over two million of them headed out for the Promised Land of Canaan, but after such a victory there was another issue up around the river bend. (Pocahontas reference).

Exodus 14:1-4 shares, "Then the Lord said to Moses, "Tell the Israelites to turn back and encamp near Pi Hahiroth, between Migdol and the sea. They are to encamp by the sea, directly opposite Baal Zephon. Pharaoh will think, 'The Israelites are wandering around the land in confusion, hemmed in by the desert.' And I will harden Pharaoh's heart, and he will pursue them. But I will gain glory for myself through Pharaoh and all his army, and the Egyptians will know that I am the Lord." So the Israelites did this."

What this means is that the original planned route was altered so that it would become more difficult, but God was setting them up for a miracle. Pharaoh's heart was heated, and he decided not to just let over two million slaves leave, not after all the plagues Egypt had seen trying to hold on to them so firmly. Moses lead the caravan of these two million people and they found themselves at the banks of the Red Sea. Now, the Red Sea is no tiny pond one can wade through or hop over, it is a massive body of water. To make matters more difficult, an entire army of hot-headed Egyptians were on their tails. The Israelites had been all grown up as slaves, so they had no idea how to fight an army. They saw the choices before them to drown or die by the sword. They felt abandoned.

How often are we too metaphorically in this spot? Where it seems there is no possible way out or option in which we come out the other side? At times, we may even find ourselves screaming at God for He was the One Who led us down this marked path and now everything is in disarray. Perhaps we saw the first leg of success and rejoiced in HIs faithfulness just to turn around and everything looks ten times worse than before. You are not the first ones to feel such feelings. The Israelites even asked if the sole reason God brought them out to the desert was because there was more room for graves out there? But God wasn't finished yet.

Moses was the leader of this group at the time, and he took orders from God. Moses knew God, He had seen His power and His sovereignty in his life, so he knew there would be a way out. He assured the Israelites to, "Moses answered the people, "Do not be afraid. Stand firm and you will see the deliverance the Lord will bring you today. The Egyptians you see today you will never see again. The Lord will fight for you; you need only to be still.".". (v. 13-14). Then God came through. Just as everything looked as hopeless as ever, God came through. He told Moses to merely lift his arm (which I'm sure Moses was very confused with) and then before their eyes the Red Sea parted.

The entire group of two million people walked across not in mud, but on dry land. On each side was a sky scraper of water as they passed through the waters. Then as the Egyptians attempted to cross, the waters fell upon them and they were wiped out. God took care of each and every single one. He kept true to His word that not only would the Israelites see Who God was, but so would the Egyptians. God protects His own.

God is never changing, His character remains steadfast forever, as is true in the New Testament and today as well. Jesus says in John 13:7, "You do not understand what I am doing now, but one day you will." We can also see in Romans 8:28, "And we know that in all things God works for the good of those who love him, who have been called according to his purpose."

We may not get the Red Sea parting each and every single time, but we can know that He will indeed work all things together for our good and His purpose and glory. How beautiful is that?

I write this yes as a blog, but also as a reminder to myself. Last week I found myself weeping at the banks of the Red Sea. Feeling confused and lost on this journey He has asked me to trust and follow Him in, but I realize that He came through for people who trusted and followed Him before, and He will do it again. 1 Sam. 15:29 says, "God is not a man that He should lie or change His mind," and we can hold on to that promise. He is Who He says He is, and just as His eye is on a sparrow, His eye is on us too

Prayer:

Dear Lord,

We stand here today at the Banks of the Red Sea. You led us here, just as You led the people of Israel here once too. Lord, in that day long ago You remembered Your promise, and You came through. You saved a nation that day for Your glory, and we pray that in this moment You would come through for us. Let us never forget Your promises or provisions, rather, let us hold firmly to the belief that You are working all things together for Your glory and our benefit, whether this sea parts or not.

In Jesus name,
Amen

Olive You

It has become such an unfortunate stereotype of so-called Christians that all Christianity is about is a bunch of angry, judgmental people with a righteous attitude. What they neglect to understand is that the Bible is completely full of fallen and very much human people just like you and me. I could rant for hours upon this subject, but for this post I'd like to dive a little into a certain Psalm David poured out.

David was renowned for being a man after God's own heart. From a young age he stood in faith to defeat a literal Giant with a mere slingshot and as a teen was told that he would be King, albeit he did not feel he deserved to be so. His life was full of uncertainties throughout, but what is most compelling is his heart throughout the Psalms.

The Psalms for the most part were penned by David, many of them are songs full of ever changing emotions...I certainly doubt I am the only one who can relate. One of the most incredible Psalms is Psalm 52,

> "But I am like an olive tree
> flourishing in the house of God;
> I trust in God's unfailing love
> for ever and ever.
> For what you have done I will always praise
> you

in the presence of your faithful people.
And I will hope in your name,
for your name is good."

In all of creation, the olive tree is one of the longest living and enduring trees. David felt like an olive tree flourishing in the deep roots of God. Christ speaks of the meaning of roots later in Mark 4:8, "Still other seed fell on good soil. It came up, grew and produced a crop, some multiplying thirty, some sixty, some a hundred times."

Jesus speaks further of what it means to produce an abundant crop later in John 15, "I am the true vine, and my Father is the gardener. He cuts off every branch in me that bears no fruit, while every branch that does bear fruit He prunes so that it will be even more fruitful. Remain in me, and I will remain in you." What Jesus is conveying here is just like David, we are branches off the vine of Him. God is the Gardener and albeit it is very painful, He prunes us, He refines us. The seasons of this pruning are painful, tedious, and excruciating at times, but for a greater purpose. Just like an olive tree being deeply rooted in Christ, we abide in the True Vine, knowing that the seasons of pruning are not in vain. Rather, these seasons are so that in the harvest season the harvest will be plentiful.

Malachi 3:10 says, "Test me in this," says the Lord Almighty, "a see if I will not throw open the floodgates of heaven and pour out so much blessing that you will not have enough room to for it. I will prevent pests from devouring your crops, and the vines in your fields will not cast their fruit," Says the Lord Almighty. Then all the nations will call you blessed, for yours will be a delightful land."

I am not saying that we are to walk into these pruning seasons in hopes of an abundance of money, but what I do believe we walk out of such seasons with is an abundance of the Spirit within us. A closeness, an abiding, a rooting so deep within God that it is a peace unknown and unachievable by any other way.

Let us pray to be like King David, deeply rooted in Him like an olive tree. Let us pray to be a flourishing olive tree and know that the pruning seasons will bear an abundance of fruit. The fruit of peace. The fruit of love. The fruit of truth. The fruit of Holy Spirit, the greatest reward this life does not deserve.

Prayer:

Dear Lord,

Lord, make us like that of an olive tree, deeply rooted in You. Grow us, prune us, destine us to flourish for Your glory. May we stand apart from the rest of the world, so that others may see Your glory through our lives. Lord, flourish us, and be with us as we endure the pruning to Your liking.

In Jesus name,
Amen.

God's Plan vs Ours

So, you have followed Psalm 37:4 and given your heart fully surrendered to the Lord. He's planted within your heart a dream, a vision, a hope for your future. You think the path to that will be the top of this picture, but then you get rolling and slowly it becomes the bottom picture. You begin to become confused, doubtful, and possibly a little angered at all the struggles, but when if there is something greater in store than merely getting from A to B? What if climbing this mountain will prove for something far greater than reaching the finish line? What if by the end of it, you're a different person entirely? Keep with me now.....

It may be the most cliché Christian idiom in the book to compare a journey to climbing a mountain, but when was the last time anyone actually took a Saturday to hike up a mountain? One Saturday a group of us from my church went to climb Spy Rock, a four-mile hike uphill with about a 3700-foot elevation. I prayed before we left that God would teach me something this day, and boy did He ever.

We started out the morning in the pouring rain, unsure of the conditions that awaited us two hours away, but with optimistic hearts and an idealistic hope that the day would prove sunny. It did. The hike started off as a simple nature trail, but then was met with steep hills and rocks. I know it's cliché, but keep going with me with this spiritual analogy. Not going to lie, I felt winded after the first quarter mile of a steep uphill climb and was severely regretting only going to the gym three times a week this summer and not daily like I did in the Spring. Nevertheless, I kept going. Soon the trail increased and was a lot harder, steeper, more challenging. The thing was, the beginning of the trail had trained me up, so by the time I got to the more challenging spots, the beginning seemed like a walk in the park (literally). Then came the real challenge. Scaling the rock to the top.

I have taken one rock climbing class, and borderline scaled a rock once before, so this was all new. I looked up at the top and part of me wanted to give up, head back to where I began without victory, a story, or success. Something in our spirits wants to give up at the eleventh hour, doesn't it? Something within us wants to walk away even though we have endured so much and worked so hard, because of many things, but mainly we are exhausted, and we are fearful. Yet I endured.

I took it slow and steady, but I scaled that giant rock of a mountain. Taking risks and holding my breath, but then quickly I made it to the top. Gosh was it worth it.

The view was incredible, to see how far I had come, and to see all of God's glory in creation surrounding us. An untouched plethora of green cascaded the span of the sky. Suddenly being tired didn't even matter, nor did how long it had taken to get to the top. It no longer mattered that half way up all the anxiety I had experienced had happened either. Then came the best part.

Of all the things, I could ever hope to be, a bird tops the list. I envy birds to no end; their freedom, their beauty, their ability to swiftly navigate the sky and all of creation. Up there on Spy Rock I felt a bird, especially because passing through the rock was a literal cloud. We all saw the cloud hover near us and suddenly embrace us within its billowy fog. The smell

(picture by one of my students, Greyson Flores)

Reflecting later, I realized God brought me through today's experience to show me what He has done, what He is doing, and what He will do. It is applicable to just about any journey, but I knew the specifics He was pointing out for me here. The journey may start out rocky, but endurance produces perseverance and suddenly the beginning seems minuscule compared to what occurs when you're really going. That perseverance produces character when that eleventh-hour strikes, and you want to give up, when you want to turn back. And that character produces hope, hope that once you're at the top, it will all have been worth it. Indeed, it was, and indeed it will be. Worth every step, every stumble, every ounce of stamina. The greatest reward of all, is journeys create for us a chance to know Christ better. A chance to learn more about Who He really is, and what we are really made of. The greatest piece of that, is that relationship and that understanding of Him is so glorious, the view from the top pales in comparison, but is brought even more vibrantly alive by its accompaniment. Keep climbing, friend.

Prayer:

Dear Lord,

Though we make so many plans, oftentimes they are changed. We know that You see our plans and change them to in actuality, to be perfect. Lord, we give these plans and goals and aspirations to You so that You may have the control and say in our lives.

We praise You, oh Lord.

In Jesus name,
Amen

Off the Cuff Moment

Do you ever procrastinate? I do.

Actually, the main reason my first book ever happened was because my Senior year of college I as avoiding doing homework and wrote a book instead. Then I wrote an album to avoid a Senior project.

Now I'm in the workforce and sitting in my office writing this book to literally avoid writing a thank you card to a school we did development study at last week.

So, the moral of this little commercial break is that procrastination can produce books.

Under the Wing

Spiritual warfare is real. It is war. It is overwhelming. It is not hopeless. It is worth it.

In my walk as a Christian I have come to see a number of Christians who have never really experienced an attack of the enemy that was not in the form of what we commonly think of as temptation. In Matthew 4 we see Jesus being tempted by the enemy, but what did this actually mean? Mainstream culture will describe temptation in layman's terms as something we ought not to do, but are lured with a compelling carrot into nearly or actually doing. This is something the enemy will quite often whip up to distract us from our God given missions, or to fall yet again to our flesh. What is often overlooked, but actually very prevalent is the other form of temptation in attack on a person from the enemy.

These attacks were seen in Matthew 4 as well when the enemy fought against Jesus. They are seen in Daniel 10 when it recalls that the angel sent to assist Daniel took 21 days to fight through the warfare before he could reach Daniel. These attacks are packed with anxiety, fear, paranoia, and a sense of inadequacy. These attacks will seek to convince a person that God is a liar, just as the enemy attempted to convince Eve that God was fooling her. These attacks will create a cyclone of confusion and doubt swirling about as we are left clinging to the wreckage to merely breathe- all within our own heads. Below are verses to discern what is God and what is not, and how to fight back:

1 Corinthians 14- "God is not a God of confusion, but of order"

1 John 4:18- "Perfect love casts out all fears"

1 Peter 5:7- "Cast your cares and anxieties on Him, for He cares for you."

John 16:33, "In this world you will have trials, but fear not, for I have overcome the world."

Look at Job. He was actually the most upright and righteous man in the world when the enemy sought to attack his life. The enemy came to God to ask if he could attack Job, because nothing is permitted to hit us without permission, but it leads the questions, why would a kind and loving God allow this? The answer is simply: so, we lean on Him. You see, Job was attacked on everything. His livelihood in money was lost, his health deteriorated, and he even lost all of his children on the same day. I look at these and correlate them within my own life of job loss, health issues, or the loss of someone I loved more than life. Job in truth is my home-slice. As per usual of us humans, our friends always have two cents to interject. Job's friends came around him and for a period, just sat silent, unsure of what to say. Some quipped that Job must have sinned in some way, and that this was what he deserved. Others told Job to leave God entirely and give up hope. One friend had a different approach, and stated just the truth that He is a mystery, bigger than we can comprehend, so we shouldn't try to. Job felt alone, broken, confused, and like he was the last person on earth who believed God still had hope for his life. Then God showed up. The key to look at here was that it was not anything that Job earned. Job didn't burn so many sacrifices that he earned enough brownie points to capture the attention of God, nor did he figure out his life. He simply just sought God, and waited. Then God showed up.

God showed up, but He showed out too. He showed His sovereignty and power, think about how Job had a personal encounter with the Living God that created the entire Universe? He endured the storms, he clung to God, and none of it was in vain.

Not a stitch, not a tear, not a prayer in vain. Then coming like a "thunderous roar" (Job 37) God came and showed that He was there the entire time. Not a second passed without God being right there. The story has a happy ending in that God actually blessed Job double what he had before-He even paid Him back exponentially with the time, Job lived to be 140. Though money, health, and children are a blessing, Job received the greatest reward in knowing God personally.

Job isn't the only one who saw that He is our greatest reward and treasure. Hannah, the mother of Samuel, saw this first hand as well. The Bible recalls that she, "copiously sobbed" at the alter so much to the point she could barely breathe. She wanted a son, and though it was not an attack of the enemy per say, she ached and pained for this. Then God showed up, He kept His promise to her and within a short time she did indeed have her son. What is beautiful in her song in 1 Samuel 2 is that she praises God for Who He is far more than receiving what she asked for.

The beauty of trials is that in them we see what the true reward and glory is: knowing God Himself. It is of no surprise that in the same letter Paul wrote to the Church in Ephesus that there is mention of this along with gearing up for warfare. Chapter 3:16-20 shares, "That you, being rooted in the depths of God may come to know with all the saints how......." and then in Chapter 6 of gearing up to fight off the attacks of the enemy. This six sectioned letter must be seen as a whole here, and we must grasp that though these attacks come-they produce a great reward. Just as Romans 5 highlights: trials produce perseverance and endurance, which in turn produce our character, which produce hope. That hope is in Christ, that hope makes every blurry out looked tear worth it, my friends. That hope makes even laying in your closet curled in a ball copiously sobbing worth it, for we get more of Him.

Typically, if the enemy is attacking you, God has something really incredible happening behind the scenes. Don't cave. Don't walk away. Press into Him, for as it says in Psalms 91:4, "He will comfort us and shield us under His wings." He is glorified when we admit our own weakness and how desperately we need Him. He is glorified when we come to know His character better through these trials. He is glorified when we are no longer distracted from mundane life, and are given the heavy coat of burden to wear for a time so that He can take it off of us. He is glorified, and we are satisfied in Him to the point where it is not the storm ending or the potential rewards at the end; it's knowing Him more truly.

Dear Lord,

We praise You for this day. Lord, some reading this, including myself, are under attack today. We are scared and as ardently we want to think our strength is, we fall short of being able to save ourselves. We need a Savior, we need You. Lord, please be our shield and rampart. Lord, please overwhelm us with Your Holy Spirit. Cover us with Your wings, and bring us into a deeper understanding of Who You are. You are the Glory, Lord. Bring us ever closer to You.

In Your name we pray,
Amen.

Chapter IX: Bloomed

Mentoring Those Younger than You

There comes a true blessing in helping other people, and as Christians we are called to do so. This includes mentoring those younger than you. Often the word, "mentor" holds the connotation of being over sixty with long walks in the park sharing your wisdom, but in truth, it's befriending someone younger than you and sharing lessons you've learned.

Everyone has a story, everyone has learned something in their lives, and everyone can stand to learn from others. Not a single person on earth has learned everything or seen everything, and often times they can save a lot of trouble learning from others.

It's one thing to say it is important to mentor, but it's another to find those to mentor. Of course, it is important to pray, but there are ways to help find those to mentor. For example, volunteering with the youth. Even if you do not think you have something to offer, dollars to donuts something you've been through could help someone else.

The human element has become a true rarity in a world built around technology, but that makes its necessity all the more vital. We must not allow technology to steal the true essence of what our hearts are made for.

It says in Genesis 2:18 that it is not good for man to be alone, and in such we need each other. We need each other to learn from, grow from, to help. Mentoring is a beautiful ministry that embraces this, but also changes us in the process. Throughout the Scriptures we see examples of this, from Elijah mentoring Elisha, to Jesus mentoring the Disciples.

God often works in mysterious ways to provide someone to mentor you, or for you to mentor. Prayer is the key, along with discernment. A wise man once said to never take advice from someone doing worse than you, and there is much truth in that statement. Being mentored is important in that you test each and every ounce of what a person is saying against the Word of God to ensure that it is indeed of Him. In the same way, whatever you are sharing with someone you mentor should be checked according to the Will of God and His Word.

Go forward and pray for a mentor or someone to mentor. Don't shy away from it, embrace it and flourish from it.

Prayer:

Dear Lord,

We thank You for mentors and for those to mentor. Lord, just as You matched those in the Bible for such callings, we pray You would do the same today in us.

In Jesus name,
Amen

Failure to Launch: Jobs

Remember career day in Kindergarten where you had to know what you wanted to be when you grew up? At the time, it was a fun activity, but what I didn't realize was it was the precedent for what the remainder of my schooling would pertain to: what I wanted to be as an adult.

Of course, we rarely know at five what we want to spend the remaining 75 years of our lives doing, but it did get the ball rolling on thinking about it. High school became the pressing period to get into a good college, which would secure a good job, which would secure a good life. An avalanche of pressure began with the small rolling snow ball of career day.

More than likely you said you wanted to be an astronaut at five, but perhaps now are thinking of something entirely different. It depends on the age, but if you're in your final years of high school or in the midst of college, you either have no earthly idea or a firmer grasp on what you want to do. Believe it or not, people rarely end up in the profession of their major. According to the Washington Post only 27% of people who went to college ended up in a profession related to their major.

There is also the aspect of society and environment that will positively or negatively affect your future plans. Perhaps a parent or mentor will suggest a "safe" major such as business that will more than likely secure a cubicle job by 25. Recalling back, a good friend actually became a nurse for the women in her family had all been nurses for generations. Sometimes those closest to us mean well and earnestly want to impart wisdom to help us in our future ventures, but in the end, it is between you and God alone.

By nature, I am a planner. I can tell you what the remainder of my week looks like and I nearly have a virtual calendar in my head of my writing schedule for the next month...I am sadly not even joking. When it came to a career though, I was totally lost. In high school, I thought for sure I wanted to be a museum curator. Slightly (more than slightly) obsessed with the National Treasure franchise, the idea of working in a museum made my heart soar (as did Riley Poole, haha). I sought out a summer internship at a local museum and found that though it was a great summer job, it wasn't for me. College rolled about, and I changed my major multiple times. I decided on English because of a teacher I had in the tenth grade that honestly changed every aspect of how I saw writing and literature, and additionally I knew that Don Henley of the Eagles had said being an English major helped him in songwriting. After college, I still pursued my writing and songwriting, but ended up selling and fixing phones and computers for Apple. Then health issues caused me to leave Apple and I worked as a Teller for Wells Fargo.... let's just say that was basically the place where creativity, dreams, and happiness go to die. Then God kind of hit me over the head with what He wanted me to do. What I had said 20 years prior at career day: teach.

The thing is, I could have saved a lot of time going for teaching years earlier, but I do not regret a single day at other jobs. God used that time so well. Working for the museum taught me how to bring history alive to others. Apple took an extremely introverted girl and plunged her into the busiest retail store-and she grew. I learned how to talk to people, how to teach others how to use their products, and how to have a heart-to-heart connection with a stranger and step out talking about God sometimes too.

Wells taught me that I hate corporate, and that I am far too creative to be so stifled, but what it also allowed me to do was to write. I took my journal with me and scribbled down devotionals, chapters, ideas, and prayers for hours a day. I then sought out a few publications and was picked up by Polished Ministries to become the leader of their teen department. It also is what spurred this book to be picked up to write again.

God used every single job prior to prepare me for the next. When He led me to teach, nothing had ever felt so right. It all clicked and just as Elisha's servant in 2 Kings 6, God opened my eyes to see. The calling I ignored for 20 years ended up being the one thing that made me actually want to get up in the morning to do. It made me feel fulfilled and happy, even if I was making a small paycheck.

It may take years of random jobs to find what is exactly right for you, but each of those jobs are stepping stones. Each of those jobs reveal more of what you enjoy doing, and what you don't enjoy doing. In many ways, "God blessed the broken road that led me straight to you" (my lovely job!).

So now you're reading this and thinking either: yay! or, "sure that's great.... for you *eye roll*." If it is the latter, it's ok. It is ok not to know what you want to do when you grow up. I don't think many adults know what they want to do when they grow up. Even praying about it for years may result in an unanswered prayer and confusion, but fear not. God knows your heart so well that He knows exactly how to reveal yourself to you. He knows how you are wired, for He made you, and He knows how to get you to the right place.

A few "failure to launch" tips:

1) In school try any club, group, or society that interests you. If nothing else you will find a passion, hobby, or know what you hate.

2) Don't close yourself off to things that scare you. I'm not saying to join a skydiving club, but give public speaking the 'ol college try. Don't scoff at even trying out for a school play.

3) Do not let what others say dictate your life for a career. It is your life, and it's what you have to spend every day doing.

4) Happiness matters more than bank accounts.

5) Pray. Pray without ceasing. Pray with the intent to let God change your heart and direct your steps.

6) Remember Proverbs 3:5-6, "Trust in the Lord with all your heart

and lean not on your own understanding; in all your ways submit to him, and he will make your paths straight"

Prayer:

Dear Lord,

You know all things, most especially the hearts you have grown in us. Lord, please guide our paths and teach us to fully trust You, even when we do not see how or when or why. Lord, make our paths straight and make our paths so that we in turn understand You more deeply.

In Jesus name,
Amen

Off the Cuff

So, one-time Charlotte and I went to Maymont and unbeknownst to us the park closes at 5 pm, so around 5:40 we mosey over to the gate to find everything locked and closed. So, I make the pioneer venture to climb the fence and successful am teetering the top when I hear a loud voice on a loud speaker say, "DAGNABIT! You did it! I was going to bet ya $20 you couldn't and ya did!" ...the park cops found us. Laughed at me. Did not give me $20, and I tore a hole in my new jeans. And this my friends was a fantastic adventure that I sit back and laugh at in gratitude, because this is living.

Walk Fearlessly into the Future

"Fear Not" is spoken in the Bible 365 times, and as the cliché Christian coining goes, we should omit from becoming afraid every day of the year.... this is far easier said than done. Fear is inevitable in our lives, no matter how earnestly we try to become Spartans and tough as nails, we at some point will fall to fear, but we have an advocate behind us.

What does it really mean when we are afraid? 1 John 4:18 says, "There is no fear in love. But perfect love drives out fear, because fear has to do with punishment. The one who fears is not made perfect in love." So, when we don't feel loved, we feel afraid. We fear that God no longer loves us, or really, God no longer likes us, and we become fearful of the unknown. This is no surprise to Christ, He knows we are humans and that at times we will not feel that perfect love and be subject to fear. What are we to do about this problem then? 1 Peter 5:7 shares, "Cast all your anxiety on him because he cares for you." It is easy to say to cast your anxieties and fears, but what does that really mean? The act of casting out our fears is very much like casting a net out for fish, it won't always bring all we need on the first try. In that, we must cast these fears out again and again and reap in the peace each time the enemy comes knocking with that fear. Pull in the peace and trust that in the course of doing so, we are not nearly reaping peace, but we are coming into a place where we actually understand Him better.

Jesus wants to take on your problems, no really, He does. He says so in Matthew 11:28, "Come to me, all you who are weary and burdened, and I will give you rest. Take my yoke upon you and learn from me, for I am gentle and humble in heart, and you will find rest for your souls. For my yoke is easy and my burden is light." He actually desires to take on your burdens and walk with you through those dark times. The beauty is that when we are walking through those storms with Him, we actually begin to see the Light and we feel that peace, we feel loved. That love translates in our hearts and soothes the fears, bringing to truth that indeed perfect love casts out all fear. Perhaps that is the beauty from ashes in storms that rock us to fear to our core; we come to find the true meaning of love and peace in Christ.

How then can we walk without fear into the future? Proverbs 31:25 is another coffee mug verse that shares, "She is clothed with strength and dignity;

she can laugh at the days to come." What is incredible is in the direct literal translation it says, "Strength and dignity are her clothing; and she shall rejoice at the day to come" Now, laugh and rejoice are synonyms in the English language, but in context they are vastly different here. What is being conveyed is because she knows the origin of her strength and hope, she can rejoice in the days to come. Yes, there will be difficult days to come, but in holding firm to that faith in God, we can walk fearlessly into the future. We can declare with the utmost confidence that we are no longer slaves to fear, for we are children of God, for we can dive into that perfect love.

Prayer:

Dear Lord,

We know fear is not of You, and in that we pray that Your perfect love would in turn cast out all fear we have. We pray that You would cleanse us and guide us in the way that we should go, fearlessly into the future. We pray that You would overwhelm us with Your peace that goes beyond all understanding.

In Jesus name,
Amen

Meal Planning

Perhaps it's a bit of a trendy thing to do, but yeah.

Meal planning believe it or not is a very adult thing to do, but more than anything it's a healthy thing to do. We buy into this fallacy that we can eat junk and keep on going without repercussions. I remember being in college where I literally would drink a 12 pack of diet mountain dew a DAY.....yeah not so good on me. After college, I gained 10lbs out of nowhere, realizing my metabolism didn't remain the same as even a year before. So here are some meal planning tips:

1) Don't go overboard with having to make it vegan, whole 30, or gluten free.

2) Craft a budget first, and learn coupons are your friend.

3) Pinterest meals that can use all of your supplies, like using leftover hamburgers in meat sauce for spaghetti night.

4) Fruits and veggies can be your friends, and don't swell the calorie count.

5) Take a serious look at calories, carbs, and especially sugars, they add up quickly and that is where the extra digits on your waistline are going to come from mainly.

6) Don't totally cut out fun foods, everything in moderation, plus a little chocolate is good for the soul sometimes.

7) Make food ahead of time, have overnight oats ready for breakfasts, or make a hot dish for the fridge that only requires to be popped in the oven.

8) Create a calorie budget for the day, plan the meals, and plan the snacks. You won't feel deprived or punished if you get snacks, but everything has a good and solid budget then too.

9) Beware fad diets or yo-yo diets that usually gain back the ten pounds you lost after going off the diet.

10) Go organic when you can, especially with milk, eggs, or meat. It's worth it and the lack of harmful hormones will pay off over time.

Below are some of my favorite recipes that you may enjoy!

"Whatever Floats Your Zucchini Boat"

Yield: 12 boats, about 6 servings

Prep Time: 15 minutes
Cook Time: 15 minutes

Ingredients
6 small zucchinis (2 1/2 lbs.)
1 Tbsp. olive oil
1 clove garlic, finely minced

Salt and freshly ground black pepper

1 cup marinara sauce (I used Classico Four Cheese)

1 1/2 cups shredded mozzarella cheese (6 oz.)

1/3 cup finely shredded parmesan cheese (1.4 oz.)

1/2 cup mini pepperoni slices

2 Tbsp. chopped fresh oregano

Instructions

Preheat oven to 400 degrees. Line a large rimmed baking sheet with parchment paper or a Silpat liner, set aside.

Cut each zucchini into halves through the length (if they don't lie flat trim a thin portion from bottoms so that they will lie mostly flat. I only had to do this with one of them). Pat insides dry with paper towels (cut portion). Align on prepared baking sheet. In a bowl, stir together olive oil and garlic then brush lightly over tops of zucchini. Sprinkle with salt and pepper to taste then brush a slightly heaping 1 Tbsp. marinara sauce over each zucchini, leaving a small rim near edges uncoated. Sprinkle tops evenly with mozzarella cheese then with parmesan cheese. Top with pepperoni slices (placing them more near centers as the cheese will melt and spread). Bake in preheated oven 12 - 18 minutes (bake time will vary depending on how thick your zucchini is and how crisp/tender you want them).

Remove from oven and sprinkle with chopped fresh oregano. Serve warm.

Midwest is Best Hot Dish

Ingredients
- 1 pound ground beef
- 1/2 c. onion, chopped
- 1 c. celery, sliced
- 1 c. carrots, sliced
- 1 c. wild rice, rinsed well
- 3 tbsp. soy sauce
- 2 c. cold water
- 1 can cream of mushroom soup
- 1 can cream of chicken soup
- black pepper, to taste

Instructions

Preheat oven to 350 degrees. In a large skillet, brown the ground beef and onions until beef is no longer pink. Drain excess grease.

In a greased 9x13 baking dish, combine celery, carrots, and wild rice. Add ground beef and onion mixture next. In a bowl, combine water, soy sauce, pepper and soups. Pour over other ingredients and mix well. Bake for 1 hour and 30 minutes.

Southern Belle Potato Salad

Ingredients

Servings: 6-8

2 1/2 pounds medium red-skinned potatoes, washed, with bad spots cut out (about 7-8)

1 teaspoon BENTON'S TABLE TASTY (or salt if you don't need low sodium)

1/2 cup mayonnaise (I used Woodstock organic)

3 tablespoons Rick's pickle relish with juice (or other sweet, high-quality)

1 1/2 tablespoons Dijon mustard

1 teaspoon sugar

1/4 teaspoon freshly ground black pepper plus more

5 large hard-boiled eggs, just the yolks folks

2 tablespoons chopped red onion

2 tablespoons chopped flat-leaf parsley

Paprika

Cut the potatoes into quarters, cover with water and simmer until tender when pierced with a knife, 20–30 minutes. Drain. Place potatoes in a large bowl and let cool slightly.

Meanwhile, whisk mayonnaise, pickle relish, Dijon mustard, sugar, 1/4 tsp. pepper, and 1 tsp. Table Tasty in a small bowl for dressing. Add onion and parsley.

Using a large wooden spoon or potato masher, coarsely smash potatoes.

Add egg yolks to potatoes and coarsely smash them together. Then gently mix in the dressing. Cover and chill.

I Just Can't Wait to be King

One of my all time favorite movies is, The Lion King, and one of the most memorable scenes is where Simba is singing as a cub how he cannot wait until he is grown and able to become king. Isn't that true of all of us? Makes me think of being a young teen and being so darn excited to drive, have a bank account, have a job and make real money, all to find that once I stepped into that adult realm.... I wanted to revert back.

There are so many perks to growing up, and freedoms that come like driving and the ability to make decisions for yourself, but at the end of the day, it really does come back to the need for guidance. You can be 17 or 77, but you still need guidance. This is where the Lord really does become your best friend yet again.

There's a verse in Jeremiah 6 that says, "This is what the LORD says: "Stand at the crossroads and look; ask for the ancient paths, ask where the good way is, and walk in it, and you will find rest for your souls." God took me here when I was praying about teaching actually. Gosh this verse rings truth. If you note, it mentions the ancient paths, so this reminds us that we are not the first ones to question what path to take. It's almost a beautiful burden how many options we have these days and paths we could take.

So, to keep this chapter short and sweet: ask God. Ask God, and follow His path. It may be scenic, it may require daring faith, it may appear completely impossible, but following Him is never a bad idea. Faithfulness is always rewarded, just not always on our timelines. But He is faithful, and He has a plan. You may just end up being glad to be you in the end too.

To quote Star Wars, "stay on target, stay on target...."

Chapter X: The One

DEAR YOUNG SPARROW / 261

At Last

"You're too picky, this is a nice Christian boy, you should be with him."

"What are you waiting for? Just choose a guy and go for it."

"Your ideals are too high, God doesn't care who you marry."

Lies. All of these are things that our society, completely obsessed with instant gratification, gravitates towards. I cannot even begin to tell you how many weddings I have been to over knee jerk reactions and crossed fingers that they were making the right decision. What if instead of grabbing the first one we can get like a sweater on black Friday that you later come to question, we take a step back? What if we are patient and we, wait for it, let God choose? What if He does care about our lives-including our love lives-and we let Him take the lead? What if we stop fearing waiting? What if there really is a moment where everything comes to a forefront and we at last see? Stick with me here.......

In all of human history there has only ever
been one recorded perfect marriage, well...perfect for
a time. You see, the first marriage was between
Adam and Eve, and before that dirty rotten Serpent
showed up, everything in the garden was perfect.
That means that their marriage was perfect, and it
was an idea of God. See, Church culture will make
you feel guilty for wanting marriage. It will make you
feel like a horrible sinner for wanting someone to
share your life with, but the truth is God designed
man not to be alone, and for the mass majority of
men-He designed for marriage. Now of course there
is the very vital and pertinent aspect of what a godly
and healthy marriage looks like with God as the
head, but for this little thought we are just going to
focus on the beginning. So, let's start at the
beginning.

"The LORD God placed the man in the Garden
of Eden to tend and watch over it. But the LORD God
warned him, "You may freely eat the fruit of every
tree in the garden— except the tree of the knowledge

of good and evil. If you eat its fruit, you are sure to
die."

Then the LORD God said, "It is not good for the
man to be alone. I will make a helper who is just right
for him." So, the LORD God formed from the ground
all the wild animals and all the birds of the sky. He
brought them to the man to see what he would call
them, and the man chose a name for each one. He
gave names to all the livestock, all the birds of the
sky, and all the wild animals. But still there was no
helper just right for him.

So, the LORD God caused the man to fall into a
deep sleep. While the man slept, the LORD God took
out one of the man's ribs and closed up the
opening. Then the LORD God made a woman from the
rib, and he brought her to the man.

"At last!" the man exclaimed.
"This one is bone from my bone,
and flesh from my flesh!
She will be called 'woman,'
because she was taken from 'man.'"

This explains why a man leaves his father and mother and is joined to his wife, and the two are united into one.

Now the man and his wife were both naked, but they felt no shame." (Genesis 2)

Gosh, there is a lot in here to chew on, so let's start a chomping. God made Adam, and He saw that it was not good for him to be alone. From the start, we see that man is 1. Made for God and 2. Man is made for each other. So, God makes every animal and asks Adam to name them all. Adam seems pretty content in this perfect paradise of a garden, a bachelor pad of sorts, along with all the (party) animals. He has a perfect relationship with God and there is still something that God says needs to be added. So, Adam waits. Not only does he wait, he naps. He literally naps people, and when he has had his long slumber, God wakes him up. Let me say that again, God wakes him up, gets his attention, tells him when to look up. What does Adam say the first time he sees his wife? Is it, "oh, well, this chick is here and it's good enough I guess." NO! He says, "at last." Ladies, swoon over this, imagine if your future spouse was so focused on God and willing to wait that only when God revealed the truth he would look at you and say, "at last." Now wouldn't that be worth the wait? Wouldn't that be something sustaining and beautiful to hold out for?

In this time and place when this story occurs, their union is 1. Holy 2. Sacred 3. Perfect. God designed every single aspect of this union, and He will do that with your love story if you let Him. Stop taking the first exit you see and let God drive. Be so focused on God and all He has called you to that until He says it is time for you to wake up, you'll keep trusting Him. You will keep focus on Him and the things He has asked you to do in the meantime-even if it is literally naming animals. When the time is right, He will reveal it and your heart and all of heaven will rejoice in proclaiming, "at last."

Prayer:
Dear Lord,

We praise You for Your time spent on us, knowing us through and through as You speak about in Psalm 139. Lord, we pray that just as You know our hearts, You would highlight to us when the time is right our very own at last moment. We pray that this moment would be eye-opening, but most truly gloriously praising to You above all else.

In Jesus name,
Amen

Bone of My Bone?

What did Adam mean in that section above where he called Eve the, "bone of his bone" really? Genesis 2
says,

""This one is bone from my bone,
and flesh from my flesh!
She will be called 'woman,'
because she was taken from 'man.'"

What he was saying was the she was his people. In today's terms, we might say that we've found our Friends "lobster" or our mate. I love the imagery given in Isaiah 34, "None of these birds will be missing her mate. For it is His mouth that has given the order, and His Spirit will gather them together." God bringing these two of a cloth together in Him. God is the One Who brings these people together, not man. Adam knew this, and he saw because God allowed him to know and see. See, Jeremiah 33:3 shares that if we are without revelation on something, to earnestly seek God and He will give that revelation. That is what happened here, God gave Adam that knowledge. He knew that this woman standing before him was the one. She would be the one cut of the same cloth. In modern terms, she would be the one who would obsess over Star Wars with him, build a giant nest as a tree house to have Bible studies in, talk about the Civil War for hours on end, get McDonald's at midnight with him just for fun. She would be his people, and he would be hers. Isn't this a beautiful thought? A beautiful hope? A beautiful desire for God to fulfill?

Now, this is not to say that God was not or is not enough, because He is. He always is more than enough, but we must recall that God said it was not good that man was alone, and that is why He made a helper suitable for him. God made man for Himself and then each other. When those two things are in the proper order, that is where abundance is the air and fragrance of the Garden.

The more we dive into the Bible and stop to just soak in the beautiful language of it all, the more we can come to see that it is a beautiful representation of His love over us. God is the Author of all these words, and we can see those words carried out in our own lives.

Bone of my bone will look different for everyone. For some it may be as simple as shared interest in puns or Star Wars or a sport. Let your walls down and you may just come to find that in fact He has more than you knew you ever wanted right there. Waiting all along for you.

Prayer:

Dear Lord,

We praise Your Holy Name. We thank You for our quirks and enigmatic tendencies, and Lord we pray that You would help us to rejoice in those beautiful rarities in our spouses. Lord, we know that no two snowflakes are alike, just as no two people are alike. We thank You for such truths, and we pray that we rejoice in those bone of my bone moments.

In Jesus name,

Amen

What to Look for in a Man

The list. Oh, the list, the list, the list. For as long as I can remember as a teen and beyond there have been suggestions of a list of qualities to pray for in a husband. Oh sure, we start these lists around thirteen years old and we say the canned answers we think we should write, but then we slip in or secretly hope he also has deep eyes. We secretly hope he's got strong arms to defend us. We secretly hope he looks like Riley Poole from National Treasure (oh wait, that's just me). The thing is, it is good to know what you want, but it's even better for God to show you. Let's go a little deeper to what that all means...

God made your heart. Psalm 139:16 says,

"You saw me before I was born.
Every day of my life was recorded in your book.
Every moment was laid out
before a single day had passed."

God knows you. He knows you best, because He made you. Let that really fill up your mind, that God made y-o-u. In that He knows what makes you happy, He knows what will be difficult for you, He knows the things you don't even know you want. All that being said, trusts Him on the spouse front. There are aspects that we should dive into the Word for to look for in a spouse, traits like honesty, a godly leader, a man after God's own heart, but let Him surprise you with other little idiosyncrasies. Make your list an outline of what a man after God's heart is, and then let Him fill in the extra lines. He knows your heart, and He won't leave you disappointed. Isaiah 49:23 says, "Then you will know that I am the Lord; those who hope in me will not be disappointed." God won't leave you disappointed or high and dry. He knows your heart, and He knows what you need most.

In the same way, we should strive to be the kind of women that honor God most. If we desire a husband that is God's highest and best, shouldn't they be receiving a wife that is God's highest and best too? How do we do this?

For starters, we work to become the Proverbs 31 woman, not for our husbands, but for God.

We are woman created by and for the most High God, and our days waking this earth are not in vain. That being said, it is so very vital that we live out each and every day in His glory. The next book will go into what being a Proverbs 31 woman really looks like, but spend time in prayer and meditation over what being that kind of woman for God looks like now. Don't let this day be in vain.

Prayer:

Dear Lord,

Thank You for brains that can discern what is right and wrong. Lord, please mold our hearts to Your will over our lives so that we may in turn glorify You. Mold us to desire what You desire for us, especially in men. Lord, guide our hearts, minds, spirits, and eyes to see what You see.

In Jesus name,
Amen

All the Feels

One of the biggest lies church culture tells us is that it is wrong and sinful to desire our spouse. The culture of the church has become so fearful that they have gone to a directly sinful nature when it comes to sex. Ephesians calls for husbands and wives to submit to each other, always looking out for the best interest of the other in love. It says in Song of Solomon to, "not awaken love until it so desires" and we must hold very conscious and firm to this. The most important aspect of this is taking it to God, not allowing anything to get out of hand. CS Lewis remarked that, "you are not a body with a soul, you are a soul with a body." Our bodies biological desire carnal desires. It is science, but the thing is we have a soul that dictates the body. This free will of the soul is intended to be given to the One Who made it for proper use really. In leaving at the throne of the cross all of this, He helps us. Proverbs 21:1 says, "The Lord directs a man's heart like a water course" and Isaiah 48:17 shares that, ""I am the Lord your God, who teaches you what is best for you, who directs you in the way you should go." We live in a fallen world, so it is evident that indeed we will fall short at times. Temptations will come. It is more common place for men to be the ones said to have an issue with temptations, but in reality, it is a common issue for women too. It rests that we cannot do this on our own accord. We are not above falling into sin without the help of the Lord. But after marriage, it is alright to have such feelings for our spouse. When God presented Eve to Adam, the first thing he said was, "at last."

Let us dwell upon what a beautiful statement that was. God gave them two commandments, first to have Him and only Him as their God, and second to go and enjoy each other. God and be fruitful and make little children that would honor Him too. From the very start it was His intention that we embrace such feelings and in the context of marriage enjoy them. The entire book of Song of Solomon is based upon this. Do not feel discouraged by what the broad spectrum our culture shares, instead, go directly to the Word, the undying and solid Absolute Truth of God for what He intends for such feelings.

Prayer:

Dear Lord,

Like a river, you can determine the course of a man's heart. Lord, please direct our hearts, minds, and spirits according to Your will. Lord, let us richly and deeply feel what You desire for us to feel so that we may in full experience know You and the plans over us.

In Jesus name,

Amen

Off the Cuff

I started this new thing called, "Cycle Bar" which is basically a form of Soul Cycle. I go and cycle every time for about 45 minutes or so. To my chagrin I only was burning 200 lousy calories per class until one night when there was an instructor named Danny. I checked my emailed calorie counts burned and it was at 400! In a glorious glee I yell out, "I LOVE DANNY!!" All to turn around and he's standing right there. Behind me. Kind of scared of me. Way to go me......but hey it was 400 calories!

Chapter XI: The Call

Epilogue

So where do we go from here? What is next on the agenda? After you leave this little coffee sesh, what are you going to do?

We live radically. We live in such a way that others see Him through us. We choose to not merely fall victim to the pitfalls of society, or the gaps in Church culture logic and we live each and every day in such a way that we pick up our cross daily and follow Him.

This requires obedience, but as it says in 1 Samuel 15:22, "It is better to obey than sacrifice." This requires being unpopular at times, and perhaps even losing friends. Jesus knew this, and in John 15:18-19 shares, "If the world hates you, understand that it hated Me first. If you were of the world, it would love you as its own. Instead, the world hates you, because you are not of the world, but I have chosen you out of the world." He has chosen **you** out of this world, so do not see being a Christian as a mark of shame, but as a badge of honor when you are rejected from this world. Know that He has greater plans for you than what you may even think, for those plans are to be of the Kingdom. What a beautiful thing when our efforts pour into the enduring glory of the Kingdom, and what an honor to be a part of such a duty.

Stand tall, stand firm, and stand out for Christ. Start each and every morning covered by His guarding feathers (Psalm 91) and gracefully go out into the world to stand for Him.

I'm praying for you, young sparrow.

Acknowledgements

Editor: Ryan Johnson

Contributor writer: Allissa Thayer
A lovely woman of faith I am blessed to call a
fellow sparrow <3

Cover Art: Megan Goss

Illustrations: Greyson Flores

All names have been changed to protect the
identities of those involved.

Sources

Chapter I:

John 13:35

Mahatma Gandhi

Hebrew 13:8

1 John 4:8

Job 12:7-10

John 15: 1-27

1 Samuel 15:29

Matthew 7:7

Jeremiah 33:3

Matthew 11:30

Meriam Webster Dictionary

CS Lewis

Mark 4:35-41

DT Nikes

1 Samuel 2

Luke 1:45

Romans 8:13

Luke 9:23

Isaiah 48:17

Psalm 37:4

Isaiah 49:23

Chapter II:

Romans 8:28

Psalm 134

Proverbs 3:5-6

Ephesians 4:32

Isaiah 51

Hosea 6:1

Relient K

Image from

http://www.flickriver.com/photos/terrible2z/17

69319719/

Chapter III:

Ecclesiastes 3:1

James 1:7

Malachi 3:10

1 Corinthians 15:33

Ecclesiastes 4:9

Angela Thomas

Chapter IV:

Matthew 25

Micah 6:8

Mark 10

Chapter V:

Matthew 7

Matthew 5

CS Lewis

2 Corinthians 12

Psalm 139

Jeremiah 6:16

Song of Solomon 2:7

Elisabeth Elliot

John Piper

1 Corinthians 13:4-7

Ephesians 3:20

Elvis Presley

Chapter VI:

2 Corinthians 6:14

Ephesians 5

Romans 8:28

John 15

Hosea 6:1

Romans 5

Romans 8:28

Genesis 2:5

Chapter VII:

Matthew 13

James 5

Air Bud

Book of Ruth

Chapter VIII:

Genesis 2

1 Corinthians 7:34-35

Mark 6:48

Eric Metaxas

Mark 4:8

Malachi 3:10

Exodus 14:1-4

John 13:7

1 Samuel 14:29

Psalm 52

John 15

Psalm 37:4

Matthew 4

Daniel 10

1 John 4:18

1 Peter 5:7

John 16:33

Job 37

Psalm 91:4

Chapter IX:

Genesis 2:18

2 Kings 6

Proverbs 3:5-6

1 John 4:18

1 Peter 5:7

Matthew 11:28

Jeremiah 6

Chapter X:

Genesis 2

Isaiah 34

Friends

Jeremiah 33:3

Psalm 139

Song of Songs 2

Proverbs 21:1

Isaiah 48:11

2 Corinthians 6:14

John 1

Chapter XI:
John 15:18-19

Biography

Cally Logan is a History teacher and writer for Polished Living Ministries. She is a small group leader for High School girls, and enjoys challenging her students to develop deeper relationships with God and to live fearlessly. She received her B.A. Degree from Regent University. In her spare time, she enjoys spending time in nature, gardening, baking, and binging Netflix. She is secretly a bird pretending to be a human.

"In life, be a snowflake: leave a mark, but no stain."

Check out her Podcast and Blog Channel at DearSparrows.com

Website: DearSparrows.com

Instagram: CallyLogan

Twitter: CallyLogan

Made in the USA
Monee, IL
27 February 2021